HEALING FROM POST-TRAUMATIC STRESS

A WORKBOOK FOR RECOVERY

HEALING FROM POST - TRAUMATIC STRESS

A WORKBOOK FOR RECOVERY

MONIQUE LANG, LCSW

McGraw Hill

New York Chicago San Francisco Lisbon London Madrid Mexico City
Milan New Delhi San Juan Seoul Singapore Sydney Toronto

Library of Congress Cataloging-in-Publication Data

Lang, Monique.
 Healing from post-traumatic stress : a workbook for recovery / Monique Lang.—1st. ed.
  p. cm.
 Includes index.
 ISBN-13: 978-0-07-149422-9 (alk. paper)
 ISBN-10: 0-07-149422-7
 1. Post-traumatic stress disorder—Patients—Rehabilitation—Handbooks, manuals, etc.
 2. Post-traumatic stress disorder—Treatment—Handbooks, manuals, etc. I. Title.

 RC552.P67L35 2007
 616.85′2103—dc22   2006103342

1 2 3 4 5 6 7 8 9 0 DOC/DOC 0 9 8 7

ISBN-13: 978-0-07-149422-9
ISBN-10: 0-07-149422-7

Interior design by Monica Baziuk

McGraw-Hill books are available at special quantity discounts to use as premiums and sales promotions, or for use in corporate training programs. For more information, please write to the Director of Special Sales, Professional Publishing, McGraw-Hill, Two Penn Plaza, New York, NY 10121-2298. Or contact your local bookstore.

This book is printed on acid-free paper.

To all the people who have had the courage
to share their stories with me and have taught me about
the impact of trauma and the resilience of the spirit.
May you walk in beauty always.

Contents

Acknowledgments

To all of you who have believed in this project, who thought I could actually do it, who have helped me with ideas, editing, prodding, pushing, expertise, and love; you know who you are, and how grateful I am.

Introduction
How to Use This Book

"Don't push the river; it will flow by itself."

Healing from Post-Traumatic Stress deals with trauma and its aftereffects. Its format loosely parallels the flow of therapy sessions as I endeavor to assist you in understanding your reactions, thoughts, feelings, and behaviors during and after your trauma. My aim in this book is to help you accept and honor any thoughts and feelings that you might have and to facilitate a return to normalcy in your life.

This book is a combination of narrative, information, and exercises. Although the format follows the general rhythm of a counseling session, it is not a replacement for professional help. Some of the information offered in this book comes from the literature on trauma. However, most of the information and exercises are derived from my work with the men and women who have shared their thoughts and feelings with me in counseling sessions. The case studies that I include are composites of my clients, and all names have been changed. In the exercises, I include the questions that my clients found most helpful. These men and women have been, and continue to be, my greatest teachers. I am grateful for their trust, their openness, and their willingness to do the hard work of healing.

Each person is a unique being, and each trauma is also unique. Therefore, your healing journey will have its own characteristics, its own tempo. You can use this book in any way that seems appropriate for you. I recommend that you do the exercises. The act of actually doing—whether it is writing, drawing, making a collage, painting, dancing, singing, or in any way expressing your thoughts and feelings—helps to release them and facilitates the healing process. Once these thoughts and feelings are externalized, they take up less mental and emotional space in your system, in the same way that writing down your "to do" list helps you not keep thinking about it. You may, however, want to just read through the text and not do the exercises—that's fine. You might want to look at the exercises and just think about the questions posed. That's fine too.

Whether you choose to just read through the book or to do the exercises, going through this book and revisiting the circumstances of your trauma can be a demanding task. Thoughts, feeling, and memories might surface that are difficult, uncomfortable, and unpleasant.

Be gentle and compassionate toward yourself and your process. Refer to Chapter 2, "Being Kind to Yourself," for strategies on how to be gentle and caring of yourself. Go at a pace that is comfortable for you. There is no right or wrong way to do this work.

Feeling depressed, having a hard time with your relationships, not being interested in work or play, a heightened or lowered sexual drive, feeling hyper, or in some way not feeling right with yourself is a normal result of trauma. However, at times those thoughts, feelings, and/or behaviors might feel overwhelming. If you are having a hard time, it is important that you seek support from a professional. There are many counselors, psychotherapists, and clerics who are skilled in trauma work and can assist you on this journey. Getting the help you need is not a sign of weakness but an act of courage and strength.

Finally, I would like to suggest that while you are working through this book you consider the following simple guidelines:

Find a Quiet Space

It is preferable that you find a quiet, safe space to do the exercises in this book. It can be indoors or outside—any place that feels good to you and where you know that you will not be disturbed or interrupted. Turn off your phone, your cell phone, your beeper, your TV, and any other device that might demand your attention.

Confidentiality

This book is for *you*. What you write, draw, or collage in it is for your eyes only. You can allow yourself to be more honest and open with your thoughts and feelings as you do the exercises if you know that no one but you will see them. If you wish to share your process with someone else, that's perfectly okay, but it should be only if and when it feels comfortable for you. You know whom in your life you can trust with your deeper truth.

Time

Give yourself enough time—I suggest about an hour per chapter. You need time to go through the material in an unhurried way, and it is a good idea to give yourself time afterward before you return to the tasks of everyday living. If you are unable to find an hour or so at once, do as much as feels comfortable and let the rest of the chapter go until another time. There is no rush. Go at your own tempo. The healing process is gradual and cannot be hurried, just as your carrots will not grow faster if you keep pulling them out of the ground to see how large they have become.

Doing the Exercises

You will notice that most exercises ask you to write, draw, and/or make a collage. There are many other ways to express yourself that might feel more appropriate to you, and all are just as valid and helpful. Use whatever style of expression is most natural and genuine for you. I also encourage you to experiment with the other modalities offered to find out for yourself what is best for you at any given time. You might choose one mode of expression one time, another at another time. Although I recommend that you use this book to express yourself, you may also choose to keep a separate writing or art journal in which you record your experiences, thoughts, or feelings. Following are some means of expression you might choose to use:

Writing

Some people find writing a comfortable and helpful way to express their thoughts and feelings. If you are a writer, I suggest that you write in stream of consciousness: just let the words flow without any consideration for content, grammar, spelling, or form. Remember that whatever you write is meant to be private, so there is no need to censor what you say.

Artwork

For some people, drawing, painting, doodling, putting color on paper, or in some way using representational symbols is a more comfortable and meaningful form of expression. I encourage you to use this approach from a place of exploration rather than worrying about the final product. It doesn't matter what your art looks like and whether or not it is a "good" piece of work. What matters is that it be a spontaneous, intuitive expression of your thoughts and feelings. Again, this is for your eyes only, and the only judgment that you might face is your own—and you may want to give your inner critic a vacation while you work on these exercises.

Collage

Gather pictures and words or phrases from magazines or other publications; cut up pieces of paper, cardboard, ribbons, or wool; find artifacts from around your living space or in nature and glue them onto a piece of paper, cardboard, or any material that you choose to create a collage. You can add words and draw pictures or symbols. As with artwork, it is not how it looks, but how it feels that matters.

Other Modalities

There are as many ways to express oneself as there are people, and each of us will find one mode of expression more appropriate than another at each particular time. It makes perfect sense that you would want to use a different means of expression depending on how you are feeling and what it is that you need to express—a bit like not wanting the same food every time you are hungry! I believe that our inner wisdom is what guides us in choosing our modality at any given time. Following is an abbreviated list of possibilities. Let yourself find the one or ones that best resonate with you or feel most right for you at a given moment.

- Movement and/or dancing
- Sounds and/or singing
- Clay work
- Sculpting
- Wood carving
- Drama/acting
- Composing
- Playing an instrument

Finding Help

After going through a traumatic experience, looking for the kind of help that you need can be traumatizing in and of itself. Here are a few suggestions:

- Read and do the exercises in Chapter 12, "You Don't Have to Do It Alone." Ask one or more of the people you have identified as helpers to assist you with the legwork. It helps others to be able to contribute their time and efforts in helping you. Also, this way you don't have to do everything yourself. Part of your healing process might include developing your ability to rely on others, which may or may not be easy for you.
- It might take some time to find the right help. Don't give up because it's not happening immediately.
- If you belong to a religious congregation, ask the leader for recommendations. Often that person can be of help to you or can refer you to an appropriate person or agency.

- Contact a victim services organization in your area. If you google "victim services" you will be connected to a variety of sites that may be helpful. If the trauma is a result of a crime, you can contact the U.S. Department of Justice's Office for Victims of Crime (OVC) at ojp.usdoj.gov/ovc, which has a directory of crime victims' services, or you can call 800-851-3420 for referrals.
- Check with social service agencies such as Catholic Charities (catholiccharitiesinfo.org) or Jewish Family Services. They can provide you with the help you need or with recommendations for therapists, doctors, clinics, or other resources.
- If you have been in therapy before, you might want to contact that person.
- Ask someone you trust for a recommendation for the type of help that you need.
- Ask your primary physician for a referral to the appropriate person or place. Many doctors have relationships with counselors, clergy, or others they could recommend.
- Call your insurance company for a name or a list of providers in your area.
- Check with a hospital. Many will offer referrals to a variety of practitioners.
- Some police stations have connections with victim services.
- If the trauma was on a large scale such as a flood, earthquake, or bombing, disaster services will be available to help individuals cope with that particular tragedy.
- Call the Red Cross.

HEALING FROM POST-TRAUMATIC STRESS

A WORKBOOK FOR RECOVERY

Trauma and Post-Traumatic Stress

Before broaching the topic of post-traumatic stress, I would like to touch upon the definition of trauma. Trauma is an incident over which we have no control and during which we typically feel fear and a sense of powerlessness to fix or get out of the situation. Going through a trauma is hard, and healing from its ramifications takes time. Traumatic events tend to undermine and shatter our beliefs about life—that we are safe, that life has a pattern, that if we do X, then Y will happen. Most traumatic experiences are outside of the frame of our ordinary life. Some are events that happen without warning and are beyond our comprehension—for example, the destruction of the World Trade Center, a bombing, or a mass shooting. Others may have been expected or predicted but are still out of the ordinary, such as an earthquake, a flood, or a hurricane.

Other traumatic experiences result from longer-lasting difficult or dangerous situations: being trapped in a mine, being in a war, being lost or abandoned in an unfamiliar, hostile place. More common experiences, but not necessarily less traumatic, are events such as a car accident, a surgical procedure, the sudden death of a loved one, the loss of a job, or a divorce.

Some kinds of trauma are in an entirely different category: the trauma of childhood abuse or neglect, sexual abuse, and domestic violence, among others. Much of what is presented in this book will help you on that healing journey as well. In addition, I recommend that you explore specialized books that address those issues more specifically.

There are traumatic situations in which you were not powerless to make a difference, instances in which your behavior may have altered the outcome of the event in some way or in which your actions may have helped others—for example, digging a tunnel into a collapsed mine, running into a burning building to save someone, or calling 911 during a robbery or attack. These heroic actions change the impact of the trauma, but they do not prevent the ramifications of the emotional, mental, and physical aspects of post-traumatic stress. This has become more apparent as we have watched the impact that the events of 9/11 have had on first responders.

Although there are many, many thoughts and feelings that arise during a traumatic event, shock, fear, disbelief, and a sense of powerlessness are common reactions. One of the ever-perplexing questions is why people respond so differently to the same situation. Why do some people who experience a traumatic event continue with their lives seemingly unruffled, while others are affected deeply? Research is also inconclusive as to what determines behavior during the actual trauma. There aren't any specific character traits or personality structures that completely predict how a person will behave in the face of danger. The timid person may turn into a hero, while the tough one may become immobilized.

There seem to be many factors that contribute to how a person will be affected by a traumatic event. The individual's psychological health at the time of the trauma, her or his personality, whether the individual was alone or with others, whether the individual had a solid religious faith, whether the individual felt her or his behavior had an impact on the outcome of the situation, whether the individual had experienced traumatic events before, and if so, what kind. However, there does not seem to be any conclusive answer to the question.

What Is Post-Traumatic Stress?

The terms *PTSD* (post-traumatic stress disorder) and *PTSS* (post-traumatic stress syndrome) lately have come into common use. But what do they really mean? PTSD/PTSS is a cluster of thoughts, feelings, behaviors, and attitudes found in people who have gone through a traumatic experience. Each person is unique, and each trauma is different. Nonetheless, there are universal patterns that seem to encompass most people. Many similar thoughts, feelings, attitudes, and behaviors are widespread in trauma survivors. These are our system's attempt to regain a sense of normalcy, to recuperate from shock, to make sense of that which doesn't make sense, and to reorganize ourselves to a new reality.

There is also a progression of stages that most people go through on their journey to recovery. These stages are not clear-cut. It's not like accomplishing a task and leaving it behind to move on to the next. However, the stages do build upon one another, and there is a definite progression toward a return to normalcy. Each person goes through the different stages in her or his own unique way and time frame. There is no right or wrong way—just your way! Our culture tends to applaud and reward a "carry on" attitude. Many believe that it is a good thing not to miss a beat, to put aside whatever traumatic event life has dished out and proceed as if nothing had happened. The truth is that traumatic events often impact us in fundamental ways— some obvious, others more subtle; some immediate, others less so—and it takes time to recover. Four seasons, or a full year, appears to be the general time frame for a new normalcy to occur. This period allows you to go through all the usual events of your life such as holidays, anniversaries, and birthdays at least once and to work through the thoughts and feelings that this new circumstance elicits.

One of the frustrating aspects of healing from trauma is that it can feel like you are taking two steps forward and one step back. Just when you think that you're done going through a particular set of thoughts, feelings, or behaviors, something happens that throws you back to an earlier stage. This too is normal, and over time, you will return to a sense of normalcy.

Post-traumatic stress is more complex when a new traumatic event has aspects of a past trauma. It can trigger some of the thoughts, feelings, and behaviors that you experienced during the first trauma. For example, a woman who had been seriously affected by the 9/11 terrorist attacks on the World Trade Center and had returned to feeling normal found herself terrified when a widespread power failure caused the lights to go out in the city. This is an example of a typical, natural reaction to a circumstance that has elements of a past traumatic incident.

Post-traumatic stress syndrome has three main phases: the acute phase, the transition phase, and the integration phase. They represent a normal and healthy adaptation to having been in a traumatic situation.

Acute Phase

The acute phase is a cluster of mental, physical, and emotional reactions that typically occur immediately after the trauma and last a few days or weeks. During this phase, it is common for you to wonder if you'll ever be okay again. You might find yourself in a state of disbelief, feeling like you can't believe this happened to you. Many people feel the physical effects of trauma: crying, shaking, or feeling achy. It is also normal to feel scared, needy, or even disoriented during this time.

Some people appear unaffected immediately after the trauma and even for days, weeks, or months thereafter. These same people might find themselves experiencing the acute phase at a later time in response to an event that has attributes of the original trauma. Others somehow put the event behind them and continue to live their lives with little or no disruption. One way is not better or worse than another. It is what it is. Honor and accept your own process, and allow yourself to do whatever will be of help to you during each particular phase. A client of mine who had been raped in her twenties told a couple of people, went to the police, and went on with her life with little if any disruption. One day, about ten years later, she came to see me after having seen a movie in which there was a rape, and she was in full acute phase.

Aspects of the acute phase can be reawakened when a situation occurs that is reminiscent of the trauma. For example, a client of mine broke into a sweat whenever she felt velvet. Once she remembered that it was because the man who had raped her was wearing a velvety shirt, she was able to work through the feelings and was no longer so affected, although she continued to shy away from velvet.

Transition Phase

The transition phase is the time when you begin to try to make sense of what happened. For many people, this can occur within a couple of days or weeks after the trauma. For others, it may take longer, a few months even. If it lasts longer than a few months, it would be advisable to seek out some type of counseling or extra support, preferably from a professional. During the transition phase, you may find yourself questioning "what if?" and trying to make the incomprehensible comprehensible. There is a lessening of the acute symptoms. Even if the upsetting thoughts, feelings, and behaviors are still present, they are less intense than in the acute phase. During the transition phase, new thoughts, feelings, and behaviors may come to replace those experienced during the acute phase.

For example, Kate worked near the World Trade Center in a senior citizens' assisted-living facility and had to help the residents evacuate the building under great difficulty. There was smoke everywhere, people were scared, and she felt responsible for all of them. During the acute phase she smelled smoke wherever she went, even though there wasn't any, and she felt herself constantly shaking on the inside and was on constant alert. During the transition phase, Kate could tell herself that not all smoke meant disaster, although she still felt uncomfortable around that smell. She stopped shaking, and although she was still on alert, she didn't jump at every little sound. She felt grateful that she and all the residents had made it out safely, and she was beginning to feel a new sense of self-mastery. These thoughts and feelings were welcomed. On the other hand, she was angry, felt that she was not safe in the world, and found herself uncomfortable being alone. These didn't feel so good. Over time, Kate was able to conquer her difficulties, and she now lives with a heightened sense of gratitude to have her life and a sense of personal mastery that she could handle any situation that came her way.

Integration Phase

During the integration phase, life returns to a new normalcy. Strange thoughts, feelings, and behaviors are more the exception than the norm. Certain aspects of your life might have changed, or may be changing. Some of your thoughts, beliefs, concepts, feelings, and views of the world may be altered. For instance, whereas you once thought of the world as a safe place, you may now realize that the world can be a dangerous place and that people do hurt each other. At the same time, you've realized that you are more resilient than you thought you were. Overall, you feel more like yourself.

Jamie, who was caught in a flood caused by heavy rains, still gets anxious when it rains hard. She also has developed ways to calm and reassure herself so she no longer feels the panicky feeling that she had then, although the triggering stimulus is there and she notices it.

In this chapter I've endeavored to give you an overview of what trauma and post-traumatic stress are. Chapter 2 will give you ideas on how to take care of yourself while going through this workbook, in preparation for Chapter 3, in which I will go into more detail about the thoughts, feelings, and behaviors associated with post-traumatic stress and begin to guide you through the process of recognizing for yourself what aspects apply to you.

Being Kind to Yourself
Self-Care Techniques

Being caring of and gentle to ourselves can be a challenge for many of us. Even for those of us who are pretty good at it, there are those times when we forget. The purpose of this chapter is to be a reminder as well as to provide you with new possibilities and ideas about how to take care of yourself, particularly at those times when you might feel triggered or out of sorts.

What being kind to yourself and taking care of yourself means varies from person to person and from time to time. Being kind to yourself might mean going for a hike today and taking a nap tomorrow. The challenge is not only to know what taking care of yourself means to you, but doing it!

We can all come up with hundreds of reasons why taking care of ourselves is not as much of a priority as whatever else needs our attention. It is true that tasks of everyday life must be accomplished; however, you must also take care of yourself if you are to heal from physical, emotional, mental, or psychological trauma. Self-care is a vital aspect of the healing process because it allows the body and mind to reinstate and reorganize the physiological, mental, and emotional patterns that were disrupted by the trauma.

As you will learn as you go through this workbook, trauma truncates our homeostasis, our normal way of being in the world. In order for emotional repair to take place, special attention needs to be given to our mind, body, and spirit—a bit like when you have the flu you might need some extra sleep, extra covers, quiet, and chicken soup!

Self-care also lets your physical, emotional, and mental self know that it is safe to do this work. When you feel safe, you can let yourself be vulnerable and out of sorts, because there is a cushion, a safety net that will be there as you go through the healing process.

Following are several suggestions that can serve as a springboard to help you find your own ways of taking care of yourself. Check which might be appropriate for you.

☐ Take a bath or shower
☐ Go for a walk
☐ Take a nap
☐ Spend quiet time alone
☐ Call a friend
☐ Have a cup of tea or coffee
☐ Enjoy a good nourishing meal or snack
☐ Do yoga
☐ Exercise
☐ Rest

☐ Watch a movie or TV show
☐ Read a book
☐ Go outside into nature
☐ Shop
☐ Go for a ride
☐ Listen to music
☐ Cook or bake
☐ Make music
☐ Meditate
☐ Do an art project

Add any other activity that makes you feel good:

_____

List three or more activities that have felt self-caring in the past:

_____

_____

_____

_____

Copy these activities on a note card and put them in a place where you will see them often. Maybe you can use that note card as a bookmark, put it in your wallet, tape it to the refrigerator, or insert it in your date book. You can also input it in your PalmPilot or as a screen saver on your computer. One of my clients' screen saver says "Breathe." It is a reminder for her to take a moment to relax. These self-care techniques are beneficial at any time, not just when you are working on this book.

Mind and Body Calming Techniques

In this section I will introduce some relaxation techniques for self-care. Many scientific studies have shown that calming the mind and the body is effective in relieving stress, fear, nervousness, sleeplessness, anxiety, and even pain—both physical and emotional. It has also been shown that these techniques help people gain greater clarity of thought and feelings. There are a multitude of meditation and relaxation techniques. Tai chi, chi gong, and yoga are excellent. Books and tapes on all these forms are easily found in bookstores and online at places like Amazon.com and One Spirit (one spirit.com), and tai chi, chi gong, or yoga classes are relatively easy to find at a YM/YWCA or a local gym. Regardless of the form, the goal of these techniques is to quiet the mind and relax the body.

Following are several practices that may be of help to you when you are having a hard time—feeling stressed, scared, nervous, anxious, sad, or overwhelmed. If there is a particular technique that you have used over time, by all means use that one, or you might want to experiment with variations. If you don't have a routine practice, it would be helpful for you to practice a variety of techniques before you begin working through this book to determine which technique you like so you will be familiar with it when you want to use it. It is harder to learn a new practice in difficult moments or when you are stressed, so try new techniques when you are feeling okay.

All of these techniques should be done in a quiet place, either inside or outdoors, where you won't be disturbed. Ten minutes is the recommended minimum time, twenty minutes the standard. You might want to set a timer so you don't have to worry about keeping time. Finding a spot that is comfortable for you and that you use time after time enhances the practice. Your mind and body begin to recognize that place and to relax just by being there, just as you might feel hungry when you go to a restaurant.

You can use these techniques in any setting and at any time when you are in need of calm and relaxation. Nevertheless, a consistent daily or weekly practice will bring added support to you at those times when you need it. It is one of those things that the more you practice, the easier it becomes. After a while it even becomes second nature. This first technique will help you deal with the thoughts, feelings, and sensations that will come up as you try to relax.

Working with Thoughts, Feelings, and Sensations

This approach can be used with any of the following techniques, as well as on its own. While practicing a relaxation technique, thoughts, feelings, and sensations are bound to crop up that begin to engage your attention. Sometimes these are lovely and soothing, and even though in a formal meditation practice you would be encouraged to clear your mind, for our purpose at this moment I encourage you to bask in the comfort that such images bring you. However, particularly at times of stress, your thoughts, feelings and sensations can be unpleasant and can spiral into worse and worse scenarios.

One of the keys to relaxing when faced with difficult thoughts, feelings, or sensations is to learn to accept them rather than fight them. Most of us naturally try to make those unpleasant experiences go away. It is paradoxical but true that the more you try to make them go away, the more they stick, because you are giving them attention and, therefore, power. If you can acknowledge and accept these thoughts without trying to change them, they will lose their grip on your mind. Obviously, for most of us, this is easier said than done, but with time and practice you will find yourself able to do it more and more. A wonderful mantra that I learned from mindfulness practice is to bring acceptance to the difficult thought, feeling, or sensation with the phrase "and this too." In this way you acknowledge what is going on and put it in a larger context of many thoughts, feelings, and sensations. It is also helpful to then focus on something positive or pleasurable: the warmth in your hands, the sun outside, the support of your chair, the caring of those close to you.

There are many methods of dealing with negative mental or emotional activity. Following are some that people who have suffered a traumatic event have found useful. In all cases the process is to acknowledge what is happening without becoming attached to it and engaging with it.

■ When a thought, feeling, or sensation comes into your awareness, name it. For example, if you are feeling sad, scared, annoyed, worried, restless, or any other feeling that might come up, say to yourself, "I am feeling sad (or scared, annoyed, worried, or restless)," without trying to make these feelings go away or change them. If you find yourself making your shopping list, thinking about work, and so on, then label that as thinking. Simply notice and name the feeling or sensation.

■ Another technique is to acknowledge the thought, feeling, or sensation, then imagine it passing through your consciousness as if it were a cloud, so it is there and it passes.

■ Use your breath. Consciously breathe in the thought, feeling, or sensation, and on the out breath, imagine it moving out of your body. You might want to give it a color, shape, or image to help you move it out of your body and mind.

■ If what you are experiencing is unpleasant, imagine it going out of your body on the out breath, and on the in breath bring in what you need. For example, breathe out fear, breathe in calm and safety.

Working with the Breath

Sit in an upright position with your back straight but not rigid. You can sit on the floor, on a cushion in a cross-legged position, or on a straight-back chair with both feet flat on the floor. Or you can lie flat on your back with legs uncrossed. Your hands can be opened and resting lightly on your knees or thighs, or next to you if you are lying down. Gently close your eyes. If you prefer to keep your eyes open, focus lightly on an object of no great interest. Some people like to look at a candle, a flower, a rock, or the floor.

Become aware of your breath without changing it, just noticing its rhythm. Keep your awareness on your breath—breath coming in through your nostrils, breath coming out of your nostrils, or breath coming into your body, breath coming out of your body. Slowly allow your breath to become slower and deeper. You might want to think "in" as you inhale, "out" as you exhale.

You can also add words like the following:

■ Breathing in, I breathe in peace (or compassion, love, calm, hope, or another positive quality).

■ Breathing out, I let go of hurt (or anger, hate, fear, or another negative quality).

■ Or you can recite a mantra, a word that is repeated over and over. For example, repeat "love," "calm," "compassion," or "peace" as you breathe.

As you repeat these words, if you begin to have feelings that are uncomfortable or that you do not wish to have, use one of the techniques described previously for working with your thoughts. Don't worry about these distractions. Just let them pass through your mind and gently return your attention to your breath.

Working with the Body

Begin by finding a comfortable position either sitting or lying down in a quiet place. This can be indoors or outdoors. It doesn't matter where you are, as long as it is private, you feel safe there, and you know you won't be disturbed.

Start by focusing on your breathing. Breathing in, breathing out. Then begin to focus your attention on your body, starting with your feet and slowly moving up your body all the way to the top of your head, directing each part that you focus upon to relax. For example: relax your toes, relax your feet, relax your ankles . . . and so on until you reach the top of your head. Don't forget to relax your brain! If you lose your concentration and find yourself in an undesired thought or feeling, simply focus your attention back onto your body and resume going through your body from where you left off. If you don't remember where you left off, don't worry. Either start from your feet again, or pick an arbitrary place along the way. You might want to add a color, and as you relax each area fill it with a color. Don't worry about having the "right" color, just use a color that you like or one that comes up in your consciousness at the moment.

Do this exercise slowly and deliberately. When you are done, return to your breath and rest in that for a couple of minutes. Most likely there are parts of your body that are harder to relax. If this is the case, don't exert any effort, just notice the difficulty, take a breath, and go on to the next part. As you do this exercise over a period of time it will become easier.

Working with Movement

This is a technique derived from authentic movement and Kripalu yoga posture flow. A twenty- to thirty-minute time frame is preferable for this practice; however, if you don't have time, do what feels right to you. You can do this in silence or with music.

Stand or lie down in a comfortable position. Take a few deep breaths and wait for your body to move. Allow your body to move in whatever way it wants to move. In this exercise, being still is part of the movement. Do not force any movement; try to let your body move you, rather than thinking what your next movement should be.

Each session might be quite different from the others. In one you might find yourself quiet and almost not moving, while in another you might find yourself pounding on a pillow or your bed, running or jumping, or a combination of all of these.

Yoga Postures

Yoga postures are often helpful for relaxation and regrounding. Both of the following postures are meant to be gentle and create no strain on the body. If either feels uncomfortable, don't do it. Occasionally people experience tears coming up in both of these postures. That's fine. It's the body releasing tension, so it is a good thing. You might want to alternate between these poses or just stay in either position. Remember to breathe without forcing and be gentle.

- **Child pose.** This is a very gentle pose. It feels protective and safe. Get on the floor on your knees, place your forehead on the floor (or as close as it gets comfortably) in front of you, and let your arms hang loose at your sides. Let your breath be gentle. Stay there for as long as is comfortable.
- **Fetal position.** This posture also feels comforting and safe. Lie on one side of your body. Bring your knees up to your chest (or as close to it as feels good), and let your top arm drape over your knee. Breathe. Stay there as long as you want.

A Note to Remember

At the end of each chapter there is a reminder to practice self-care, and often there is a reference back to this chapter. When working on healing traumatic material, it is vital to take care of yourself. There are several reasons for this:

- The process of being kind and gentle with yourself helps your whole system to feel safer and know that comfort is available. It lets your mind know that the pain and the discomfort will not last forever.
- Creating a nurturing, soothing aftermath to hold whatever feelings have come up while going through the exercises in this workbook will enhance your healing. It also creates a safety net so you do not become retraumatized while working with past traumatic material that may feel distressing.
- Recuperation time is essential after every effort in order not to burn out. It is best for our system to have a balance of activity, whether physical or mental, with a time of rest and nurturance. Professional athletes know this well: after a day of hard workout they will have a time of rest before the next.

Use this reminder for self-care as a way to help you stay in balance, or to regain balance if you have lost it.

Healing from Post-Traumatic Stress

3

Reacting to Trauma
Your Thoughts, Feelings, and Behaviors

In this chapter we will look at some thoughts, feelings, and behaviors that are commonly experienced after a traumatic event. You are invited to use the charts provided here to track your own process. There are no correct or incorrect answers. The purpose is to provide you with a menu of responses that can help you organize and examine your own reactions and to realize that whatever your reactions are, they are perfectly healthy and normal to the post-traumatic experience.

Each person perceives and responds to trauma uniquely according to his or her particular personality and life experience. Therefore, each person's pattern is different and recuperation times vary. Nevertheless, there are some common thoughts, feelings, and behaviors associated with post-traumatic stress. The following pages offer lists of frequently encountered thoughts, feelings, and behaviors. They are not "good" or "bad." They just are.

These lists are designed to help you reflect on the thoughts, feelings, behaviors, and physical symptoms that you might have experienced, or may be experiencing now. They are also meant to reassure you that you are not the only one to have those reactions. If you are having any other responses to trauma that are not listed, simply add them in the spaces provided. There is no such thing as having "wrong" symptoms.

As you go through the lists, you might find yourself checking off contradictory statements such as "I sleep all the time" and "I can't sleep." That is absolutely typical. As individuals go through the process of integration and healing they often seesaw back and forth between opposite or unrelated symptoms.

As with all the exercises in this book, make sure that you give yourself ample time and privacy to do them. You might want to take them a little bit at a time rather than doing all of them in one sitting. Make sure to connect with someone who can be of help if you're having a hard time.

Thoughts

Much as you might wish that you could get rid of certain thoughts or change them, thoughts are seldom stoppable or controllable. For example, Jamie, whom you met in Chapter 1, was caught in a flooding creek while trying to get home with her kids. For months she kept replaying the incident in her mind over and over again and thinking, I should have left earlier. Why didn't I realize that it was raining too hard to make it across the creek? How can I trust myself? Such thoughts may feel repetitive and obsessive. You might feel that your thoughts are driving you nuts, especially when they don't make sense to you and are not compatible with your normal way of thinking.

This list provides common thoughts of people who have gone through a trauma. Indicate which thoughts you have or have had:

Thought	Have It	Had It
I'm going crazy.	☐	☐
I'm not safe.	☐	☐
What's happening to me?	☐	☐
Why did it happen?	☐	☐
I should have done . . .	☐	☐
Why did I?	☐	☐
Why didn't I? If only I had . . .	☐	☐
If only I hadn't . . .	☐	☐
I'll show them.	☐	☐

Get them!	☐	☐
Will it happen again?	☐	☐
I can't believe this happened.	☐	☐
Did it really happen?	☐	☐
I have to make sure to remember what happened.	☐	☐
I want to forget what happened.	☐	☐
If I think about it, I'll never be able to stop.	☐	☐
If I don't think about it all the time . . .	☐	☐
Why can't I concentrate?	☐	☐
No one else feels this way.	☐	☐
I have to be strong.	☐	☐
It wasn't so bad.	☐	☐
Others had it worse.	☐	☐
I can't get upset.	☐	☐
It's no big deal.	☐	☐
I can handle it.	☐	☐
I don't need help.	☐	☐
I'm fine.	☐	☐
I'll never be okay.	☐	☐
Why me?	☐	☐

Use the following space to add thoughts that you have or have had that are not mentioned here. The thoughts I have listed are just a sampling. Having thoughts not listed here does not make you weird or strange or different, it just means that I didn't happen to include them in the list.

Thought	**Have It**	**Had It**
_____	☐	☐
_____	☐	☐
_____	☐	☐
_____	☐	☐
_____	☐	☐
_____	☐	☐
_____	☐	☐

Feelings

Like thoughts, feelings can come unbidden and may seem to make no sense. Know that whatever you are feeling is within the realm of what we all have the capacity to feel. You are not alone. For example, Melissa felt terrified to drive after having been in a terrible car accident (in which, fortunately, no one was badly hurt). During the acute phase, she worried that she would not be able to control her car and that next time she would surely die. She knew that the accident had not been her fault, that she had been a safe driver for a few decades, but neither of these thoughts prevented her from feeling terrified, shaking and crying at the mere thought of having to drive. Slowly, over the next few weeks, with the help of a loving partner, Melissa ventured to drive to the end of the block, and then to the mall. Now she is driving wherever she needs to go. She does still get a small twinge of anxiety when she passes the spot where the accident happened, but it is minor and passes quickly.

Following are some of the feelings often felt by trauma survivors:

Feeling	Have It	Had It
Fear	☐	☐
generalized	☐	☐
of silence	☐	☐
of sound	☐	☐
of smoke	☐	☐
of sirens	☐	☐
of light	☐	☐
of dark	☐	☐
of elevators	☐	☐
of fire	☐	☐
of airplanes	☐	☐
of cars	☐	☐
of guns	☐	☐
of crowds	☐	☐
of being alone	☐	☐
of being with people	☐	☐
of going to sleep	☐	☐
of insomnia	☐	☐

Healing from Post-Traumatic Stress

of movies	☐	☐
of specific places	☐	☐
of being trapped	☐	☐
of water	☐	☐
of drowning	☐	☐
of choking	☐	☐
of being hurt	☐	☐
Others:		
_____	☐	☐
_____	☐	☐
_____	☐	☐
Embarrassed	☐	☐
Crazy	☐	☐
Numb	☐	☐
Sad	☐	☐
Full of rage	☐	☐
Competent	☐	☐
Glad to be alive	☐	☐
Wishing you were dead	☐	☐
Angry	☐	☐
Like you don't care	☐	☐
Loving	☐	☐
Vulnerable	☐	☐
Insecure	☐	☐
More connected	☐	☐
Less connected	☐	☐
Overwhelmed	☐	☐
Depressed	☐	☐
Responsible for others	☐	☐
Revengeful	☐	☐
In shock or disbelief	☐	☐
Guilty	☐	☐
Proud	☐	☐
Grateful	☐	☐
Spacey	☐	☐
Nervous	☐	☐

Behaviors

One of the effects of post-traumatic stress that numerous people find more difficult to deal with than thoughts or feelings is personally uncharacteristic behaviors. You might find yourself acting in atypical ways. Some of these you might actually like, others might make you feel bad. The good news is that over time you can keep the ones you like and let go of the ones you don't. In the meantime, be kind and patient with yourself.

One of my clients, Mary, a rather reserved, stoic woman, found that after her emergency operation she would cry all the time at the simplest things: commercials, a card sent by a friend, the sun streaming through her window. During the acute phase, she also felt immense gratitude for being alive and found herself telling people that she loved them, all of which she found slightly embarrassing and uncomfortable. After a few weeks, as Mary entered the transition and integration phases, she stopped crying but was able to maintain a sense of gratitude and wonder for her life that she found greatly enhanced her days. She also continued to let people know in an appropriate manner when she appreciated them and felt loving toward them.

Following are some of the behaviors commonly exhibited by trauma survivors. Indicate which behaviors you have or have had:

Behavior	Have It	Had It
Crying for no apparent reason	☐	☐
Laughing for no apparent reason	☐	☐
Having insomnia	☐	☐
Sleeping too much	☐	☐
Being more assertive	☐	☐
Being more aggressive	☐	☐
Being hyperactive	☐	☐
Being lethargic	☐	☐
Planning	☐	☐
Drinking/drugging	☐	☐
Acting promiscuously	☐	☐

Behavior	Have It	Had It
Caring for others	☐	☐
Not caring about others	☐	☐
Being self-involved	☐	☐
Overspending	☐	☐
Hoarding	☐	☐
Seeking constant company	☐	☐
Isolating	☐	☐
Taking high risks	☐	☐
Taking no risks	☐	☐
Being indecisive	☐	☐
Being more decisive	☐	☐
Acting bossy	☐	☐
Being irritable	☐	☐
Acting overcautiously	☐	☐
Being cranky	☐	☐
Feeling unable to concentrate	☐	☐
Taking charge	☐	☐
Being nasty	☐	☐
Making sure doors are locked	☐	☐
Turning off lights	☐	☐
Avoiding cars, planes, subways, mountains, water, etc.	☐	☐

Use this space to add behaviors of your own that you have or have had that are not mentioned in the preceding list.

Behavior	Have It	Had It
_____	☐	☐
_____	☐	☐
_____	☐	☐
_____	☐	☐
_____	☐	☐
_____	☐	☐
_____	☐	☐

Physical Symptoms

A common consequence of having gone through a trauma is the development of a variety of physical symptoms. Some are a worsening of already existing symptoms, others are a result of physical injuries sustained during the trauma, and others still are the body's reaction to danger. It has been well documented by Drs. Bessel Van Der Kolk and Peter Levine, among others, that our bodies react physiologically to stress even when we are not technically injured. This is due to the impact of certain brain chemicals being secreted as well as the tensing of muscles to prepare for fight or flight. If you have physical symptoms that are severe or are impeding your everyday life, such as headaches, backaches, stomach problems, pain in your extremities, or any other physical symptom that you did not have before or that has become aggravated since the accident, do check it out with a physician.

You may have sustained actual physical injuries during the event, and some of your physical symptoms may be associated with those. For example, you might have been bruised, cut, burned, shot, hit, submerged in water, stuck in a cramped position, or exposed to high heat or cold and may be recovering from those injuries. Even if you were not physically hurt during the event, however, you may have some physical reactions and responses. That is normal. It is one of the ways that the body helps us to heal from the tension that accumulates in the muscles and the organs of the body when we are under stress, particularly high stress and danger.

You may also be experiencing some physical or emotional side effects of medications that you are taking for injuries you sustained or to help you through this traumatic time. For example, antibiotics can bring about anxiety and depression. These effects pass, but they can last for as long as you are taking the prescription. *This does not mean that you should not take the medicine.* If you think that you are having a reaction, contact your doctor immediately. She or he may be able to prescribe a substitute that does not have those side effects. You do not need to be in greater discomfort than you are already experiencing. One of my clients was feeling nauseous and wired all the time and discovered that it was a result of the combination of a prescription that he was taking with a medicine that he took routinely.

It was extremely rare to have this reaction, but as soon as his physician changed the prescription he felt much better.

Do not hesitate to ask questions and take care of yourself. Also make sure that all the doctors you are seeing are aware of all the medications or nutritional supplements you are taking—even if you were taking them prior to the medications prescribed after the trauma.

Check off the physical symptoms that you have or have had:

Physical Symptom	Have It	Had It
Pain	☐	☐
All over	☐	☐
Specific parts of your body:		
_____	☐	☐
_____	☐	☐
_____	☐	☐
_____	☐	☐
Muscle tension	☐	☐
Shaking	☐	☐
Stiffness	☐	☐
Stomachaches	☐	☐
Numbness	☐	☐
Hypersensitivity	☐	☐
to touch	☐	☐
to light	☐	☐
to cold	☐	☐
to heat	☐	☐
to _____	☐	☐
Nausea	☐	☐
Headaches	☐	☐
Dizziness	☐	☐
Breathing difficulties	☐	☐
Fatigue	☐	☐
Sleepiness	☐	☐
Feeling wired	☐	☐
Loss of appetite	☐	☐

Healing from Post-Traumatic Stress

Increased appetite	☐	☐
Sweating	☐	☐
Cold	☐	☐
Insomnia	☐	☐
Stuttering	☐	☐
Others:		
_____	☐	☐
_____	☐	☐
_____	☐	☐
_____	☐	☐

Take the time to write in any other physical symptom—regardless of how minimal it seems to you. It might be an indication that you need to seek medical attention, or it might be that emotional stress is manifesting itself physically. If symptoms increase or persist, do seek medical attention. Refer to the section "Finding Help" in the Introduction to this book if you need assistance in finding the right provider.

Going through these lists may have felt reassuring, or scary, or both. Use this page to express any thoughts or feelings that may have been elicited by doing the exercises.

Healing from Post-Traumatic Stress

Write, draw, and/or make a collage of your feelings about going through the material in this chapter.

Before you go back to your everyday life, take some time to do something nice for yourself: take a walk, listen to music, talk with a friend, enjoy a quiet cup of tea, go shopping, have a massage, take a bath—whatever would feel loving to you.

Again, remember that it is a loving thing to do for yourself to seek the counsel of a group, a therapist, a cleric, or a counselor. There is no need for you to go through post-traumatic stress alone!

4

Your Story

Regardless of whether you were alone or with others at the time of your trauma, *your* experience, *your* story is different from anyone else's. Even when the circumstances are the same for many people, each person processes them differently. I'm sure that you have experienced talking with friends, colleagues, or relatives about an activity that you shared together. The way they remember it may not be exactly the same as the way you remember it, and the way they felt about it may not be quite how you felt about it. It's exactly the same with a traumatic event. Each person has her or his own perspective of what took place, and each person has her or his own feelings about it.

There are many reasons for this. Here are some of them:

- Each of you experienced what was happening from a different point of view.
- Each individual comes from a different background and life experience, which may affect her or his point of view.
- You were not physically in the exact same place and therefore didn't have the same perspective.
- Each person is different and experiences events in her or his own way.
- You might have been engaged in a different activity than the other people with you.

- There are many other reasons as well. I invite you to add to the list:

_____

_____

_____

_____

An important part of the healing process is the opportunity to tell your story, to remember and express how it was for you. You might believe that telling your story, especially if you've had to tell it before, is a waste of time or self-indulgent. However, the expression of feelings, thoughts, and physical sensations in a safe, unstructured, nonjudgmental setting serves as a tool to process events. This catharsis also serves to enhance your perspective and to decrease your feelings of fear, depression, and anger, and it allows you to knit back together the emotional pieces of your life. The reason is simple. Once you put something on paper or in some way release it through art, music, or movement, it no longer takes up as much of your psychological, emotional, or mental energy—just like if you carry your to-do list in your head it tends to preoccupy you more than when you write it down.

The following pages provide guidelines on how to tell your own story. Follow these, or create your own. Because this is a book, I have chosen forms of expression that fit within that context; however, you might chose to sculpt or dance or build or make music to tell your story. It really doesn't matter. What matters is that it be meaningful to *you*.

Another aspect of going through a traumatic experience is that it may trigger, or bring back to mind, another time or times when you were traumatized. This occurs particularly if that first traumatic incident was not fully processed, or if your memory of it was repressed or hidden. The thoughts and feelings that you had during the previous trauma might return full force. That is also normal and natural. The good news is that now is a new opportunity for healing from the earlier trauma as well. There are some extra pages available in this chapter to express whatever is brought to your mind, should you need them. And of course you can always use blank paper or canvas or whatever medium is best suited to your particular mode of expression at this time.

A Gentle Reminder

Be as specific as you can in recalling your experience without struggling or pushing to know more, remember more, or be more exact. Be aware that new details, memories, thoughts, feelings, and sensations might emerge as you begin to focus on your experience. This is normal and to be expected. If you are feeling overwhelmed, scared, or flooded by thoughts, feelings, or sensations, you can stop and come back to this chapter or this exercise at a later time. It is most important that you take good care of yourself.

Therefore, before you begin I encourage you to do the following:

- Find a safe, comfortable, quiet place where you will not be interrupted.
- Turn off your phone, cell phone, beeper, and all other distracting devices.
- Give yourself enough time to do the exercises.
- Only do as much as you're comfortable with. You can always return to a section or exercise when you are ready.
- Schedule some downtime afterward to decompress.
- Check in with someone you trust after you've done the exercise, or ask her or him to check in with you.
- Review Chapter 2 on self-care techniques.

Write, draw, and/or make a collage of what your traumatic event was.

Show in words, pictures, or symbols what the surroundings were at the time of your trauma.

Healing from Post-Traumatic Stress

Were you with others? Who else was there? What was it like for you to have those other people there? Was it helpful or not? Use words, pictures, or symbols to show who else was there with you and to describe what was and was not helpful for you.

☞ *What did you think or feel about the people who were with you at the time of the trauma? Use words, pictures, or symbols to show how you felt.*

☞ *What do you think or feel about the people who are with you now? Use words, pictures, or symbols to show how you feel.*

It is common for people who have suffered a previous traumatic experience to have some of the thoughts, feelings, and sensations that were felt then come back in the present. If you had a previous traumatic experience, how does the one you are dealing with now relate to your past experience? Take some time to describe in words, pictures, or a collage how these traumatic events are connected—or not connected.

> *Did any feelings, thoughts, sensations, or memories from your past trauma come back? What are those? Use the space below to describe them.*

_____
_____
_____
_____
_____
_____
_____
_____
_____
_____
_____
_____
_____
_____
_____
_____
_____
_____
_____
_____
_____

Congratulations! You have just taken a huge step on your journey to getting through post-traumatic stress. For so many of us, conditioned as we are to be silent about the things that impact us deeply, being able to externalize—to not have to contain—our thoughts and feelings can feel risky. It can also be deeply satisfying to be able to focus on all the aspects of your story within your own tempo, without having to hold back your feelings and sensations, knowing that no one will judge or comment.

You might want to take a moment to reflect on what it was like for you to do the exercises in this chapter. Did you remember things that you hadn't before in telling the story? Did you learn anything about yourself or recognize some qualities within yourself? You might feel relieved like Eryn, in the next paragraph, or you might feel that the telling of your story is not yet complete for you. It is all right to come back to this exercise at a later time if it feels incomplete, or you might now want to tell someone else, setting the parameters of how you want to be heard.

Eryn was referred to me because she saw someone being hit by a truck while crossing a street and die on the spot. She had already made reports to the police and had talked to some friends, but she was still quite shaken by the experience. I invited her to simply tell me the whole story from the beginning, starting from what happened before she saw the truck go over the woman's body. I also invited her to include any thoughts, feelings, sensations, and emotions that she had at the time. As she told the story, she allowed herself to cry, to shake, to feel scared and angry, to feel powerless, to fling invectives at the driver, to voice her judgment toward other people whose behavior she disapproved of, and to recognize her own presence of mind in dealing with the situation. She allowed herself to be compassionate toward herself when she felt that she had collapsed after it was all over. When she was done she gave a huge sigh and said, "Wow, that was intense! I feel that I've cleaned out all the gunk I'd been carrying since that day that I felt no one would ever want to hear—even me!"

Doing these exercises may have brought up all kinds of thoughts, feelings, and memories you wish hadn't come up. This is normal and natural and part of the healing process. Or you may have found yourself going numb: going through the exercise without much feeling, or even doing them as if you weren't fully present. That too is a natural reaction to remembering a difficult episode.

Whatever your personal response, the important thing is for you to respect your own process. Remember that there is no "right" or "wrong" way to do this. You are a unique individual, and your way is the right way for you at this time.

Find a way to care for yourself before you go on with your day. If you are having difficulties coming up with the right thing for now, refer back to Chapter 2. A counselor or therapist or cleric can also support you through the healing process. Reaching out for help is not a sign of weakness, but one of strength.

5

Fight, Flight, Freeze

Many of us are familiar with the term *fight or flight*. It refers to our immediate, automatic, visceral, knee-jerk reaction to a dangerous situation. There is a third, less well-known reaction that is as common: *freeze*.

No matter your conditioning, your background, or your strength, you cannot anticipate what your reaction will be in the face of imminent danger. Some of the bravest and strongest people will find themselves in freeze-or-flight mode, while others who might consider themselves timid will find themselves in fight mode.

We have approximately ten to twenty seconds to determine the best course of action in any sudden dangerous situation. During these seconds, we react from our "reptilian brain," an ancient, instinctual, primordial intelligence whose only focus is survival. It is the intuition provided by this part of our brain that informs us as to the best action to take to survive: fight, flight, or freeze! The apparent danger we are reacting to can come in different forms—it can be physical, emotional, or mental. A threat, or apparent threat, to ourselves or to someone we care about can have as much impact as an actual physical event—sometimes more! For example, the expletive "I'll hurt you if . . ." can be as threatening as a pointed weapon.

Here are some examples of what you might have done at the time of your traumatic experience. You might have done one or a combination of the following:

Fight	Flight	Freeze
Punched	Ran	Played dead
Screamed	Hid	Pretended to sleep
Kicked	Called for help	Stayed in one place
Bit	Other	Left your body
Other		Other

As mentioned earlier, one way is not better than another. Fighting might have gotten you hurt in some situations, while freezing might have saved your life; in other situations freezing might have increased the possibility of harm, while fleeing might have gotten you out of the situation. The long and the short of it is that whatever you did worked, because you are alive.

In this chapter I would like to invite you to look at the circumstances of your trauma, to come to an understanding of your actions and to make peace with whatever you did or didn't do. If the trauma you experienced was not a one-time event, but more of an ongoing situation such as being in a war, you might in fact have experienced all of these states at any given time, depending on the circumstances.

As with the other exercises in this book, take your time, avoid judgment, and treat yourself with the kindness that you would offer someone else. Going through this chapter may trigger thoughts, sensations, and emotions that may have been dormant for a while. As unpleasant as that might be, it is normal and natural. If you find yourself becoming flooded or overwhelmed, or if you start having flashbacks, be gentle with yourself. You might consider stopping and taking some time for yourself. Check Chapter 2 for self-care techniques. Also remember that calling someone and asking for support may be the right thing to do.

As you do these exercises, you may find that you don't remember certain details or that you don't quite know the answer to some of the questions. That's fine. Sometimes the psyche blurs details of a traumatic event. This is a healthy self-protecting mechanism. Don't try to force yourself to remember all the details. It is not necessary, and it might actually be counterproductive.

Write, draw, and/or make a collage of what you did at the time of the traumatic event. Even if you "froze," that was doing something.

This next section invites you to look at your judgments regarding your behavior at the time of the trauma. Most of us think more clearly when we are not under pressure or stressed. On the other hand, there are some people who feel that at times of danger their thinking capacities are sharper and that they make better decisions. Regardless of your situation, the following question is intended to help you put your action into a clearer perspective based on what your mental state was at the time of the incident.

What thoughts prompted your actions at the time? Write, draw, or make a collage describing your thoughts.

*⌗ What feelings **prompted your actions at the time? Write or draw them.***

Healing from Post-Traumatic Stress

In retrospect, you may feel good about your actions and reactions at the time, or you may feel not so good. You may feel that you acted bravely or smartly and may feel proud of your actions, regardless of what they were. For example, calling for help might have saved your life. On the other hand, you may feel that you did not act or react properly, that you could or should have done something differently.

As you do the following exercises, remember that you are looking back on an event in which your feelings largely dictated your actions. Most likely you were scared and felt that there was not much time to choose your action. Fear often prompts us to behave in ways that may be different than when we feel safe and have plenty of time to examine the advantages of one course of action over another.

One of my clients, who was near the World Trade Center when the planes hit, felt a sense of panic and terror and an intense need to keep running. She was running in the wrong direction from her house, but she felt that as long as she was running she was safer. After a while she realized that she had dropped her packages and her bag, but she didn't care—she felt she just needed to run. When she realized that she was going in the wrong direction, she corrected her course. But it wasn't until she reached her street and saw her building that she felt that she could stop running. In telling the story she remarked that she didn't know how she managed to run so long, but felt that there was something inside of her pushing her beyond her own endurance.

> ✎ **How do you feel about your behavior during the trauma? Check those that apply, and add others if appropriate.**

☐ Pleased ☐ Strong
☐ Proud ☐ Weak
☐ Annoyed ☐ In control
☐ Encouraged ☐ Out of control
☐ Embarrassed ☐ Other feelings:

_____

_____

_____

Sometimes we feel a certain way about how we act in the moment and have a different viewpoint at a later date. Sometimes we feel better about what we did when we examine our actions from a broader perspective. At other times we criticize ourselves for our past behavior. As you answer the following questions, be gentle with yourself if you don't feel good about your behavior at the time of the incident. Remember that you may not have had a lot of time to assess the situation and that your reptilian brain took over and did whatever it instinctively thought was the best course of action for survival. It might not have been as elegant as you might wish it had been, but it kept you alive.

How do you feel about your behavior now?

_____

_____

_____

_____

_____

_____

_____

Do you wish you had behaved differently? Do you wish you had fled when you fought? Do you wish you had fought when you froze? Do you wish you had frozen when you acted? If so, how do you think that would have been better?

_____

_____

_____

_____

_____

Healing from Post-Traumatic Stress

_____

_____

_____

_____

It is vital for you to know that you took what seemed the best course of action at the time. In retrospect and with twenty-twenty hindsight you might have behaved differently. Perhaps that would have been better, perhaps not. I think the following example is a good illustration of how our inner wisdom guides us in the moment.

A friend of mine was robbed at gunpoint in a deserted neighborhood. He quietly surrendered his wallet and was unharmed. Later on, there was a part of him that felt that he should have been more "manly" and tried to fight the three thugs that attacked him. On the other hand, he knew that surrendering had probably saved his life. After some time, he also realized that his gentle nature could be an asset, not a liability.

As time goes by, you might find yourself returning to doubting that you did the right thing at the time of the trauma. If that's so, you might want to review these pages to remind yourself that you did what was right at the time—that you are alive. You might also want to write a note to yourself or find an object that represents that positive feeling and keep it somewhere visible so that it becomes a reminder when you forget.

One issue that frequently emerges around having done the right thing is survivor's guilt. You may believe that if you had behaved a different way, someone else might have not been hurt, or not hurt as badly, or that person might not have died. I will discuss survivor's guilt in the next chapter.

Take some time to express how this exercise was for you and what your feelings are now about your actions.

Healing from Post-Traumatic Stress

You have just done a huge piece of work. Take some time for yourself to reorient yourself to the present time and situation. You may also want to do one of the "be kind to yourself" practices.

I cannot emphasize enough how important it is for you to seek out professional help if the impact of the trauma is affecting your everyday life in unconstructive or harmful ways.

6

Guilt

Although the feeling of guilt is common among trauma survivors, it is not universal. Many people go through a traumatic event without guilt. That is a good thing, and if you are one of those, by all means skip this chapter. For those who are feeling guilty, this chapter is intended to clarify the issues for you and help you shed that burden.

Guilt is an all-encompassing term with many faces. There are different types of guilt people feel, depending on whether the trauma was experienced alone or in the context of a group. Many aspects of guilt are the same—others quite different. The kind of traumatic event you underwent may also influence your reaction. For example, natural catastrophes like floods, tornadoes, or earthquakes tend to elicit less personal guilt than events such as burglaries, holdups, car accidents, or rapes. In these more personal instances, the victim has a tendency to be more self-blaming and may take on responsibility for the event. This type of guilt is characterized by thoughts such as the following:

- Why did/didn't I . . . ?
- I should/shouldn't have . . .
- I could have . . .
- If only I had . . .
- If only I hadn't . . .

Traumatic events of a less personal nature tend to elicit more "survivor's" type guilt. Here are some characteristic thoughts of survivor's guilt:

- Why her or him and not me?
- I should have been there.
- I should have . . .
- I shouldn't have . . .

Survivor's guilt refers to the guilt felt by people who were not at the scene of the event or who survived it either unharmed or less harmed than other people involved in the trauma. Survivor's guilt may include the thoughts listed here as well as some very specific to the situation or your relationship with the victim.

If you were not there, you might feel that you should have been. You might be asking yourself, why did this happen to her, him, or them and not to me? Someone I know keeps saying that he should have been at the World Trade Center with his friends during the 9/11 attack, although he had a meeting uptown that day. He's grateful to be alive, yet feels guilty that he is and they are not. Or you might feel guilty that you didn't prevent the traumatic situation. A client felt that it was her fault that her daughter got raped because she believed that if she had not allowed her to go to the school play it would not have happened.

Another complicating aspect of survivor's guilt is a sense of gratitude and relief. Often survivors will feel thankful that they are not dead or hurt in the way that others were. One of my friends still berates himself for feeling grateful that he made it out of Vietnam alive and physically uninjured when so many of his companions didn't.

Was it possible for you to have acted differently during the trauma? Everything looks different with twenty-twenty hindsight. Looking back, you might think that you could have acted another way or made different decisions that would have altered the outcome of the trauma. But remember from Chapter 5 that in a crisis we behave instinctively in what seems to be the best possible manner to ensure survival at the time. Whatever course of action you chose was the right tactic for you at that time. If you were not directly involved in the situation, there is even less possibility that you could have done anything different than what you did.

It is possible that you might have handled yourself differently. However, beating yourself up for what you did or did not do doesn't serve you well—or anyone else for that matter! It just superimposes an extra burden on what you are already dealing with.

Some people believe that because they, or someone close to them, have suffered a tremendous loss they should not have pleasure in life. They believe that in order to pay homage to that loss they need to be miserable themselves. Actually, nothing is further from the truth. The best way to honor a person's life, whether the person has died or has been incapacitated, is to live your own life fully with integrity in a way that would make him or her happy. Going on to have a good life is not a negation of your sadness and loss, but an acknowledgment that life needs to be lived.

A lovely deed could be to create a memorial to the person. It can be simple: a scrapbook, a song, a garden, a jog, something you do that is dedicated to her or him. The other day, as I was taking my daily walk, I noticed two women who were clearing a little patch of neglected dirt at a crosswalk. I stopped to express my appreciation for their effort, and one of them volunteered that they were doing it in honor of a friend of theirs who had died. Then I noticed the plaque: "For Jack, who loves nature."

Survivor's guilt might evoke other aspects in your life where you feel guilty. This is a wonderful opportunity for you to examine those situations or relationships and to become aware of whether the guilt that you carry is appropriate or not. If the guilt that you feel is valid because you have not acted in a good way, it is an opportunity to make amends or fix the situation.

The purpose of the following exercises is to help you clarify for yourself what it is that you feel guilty about and to alleviate that burden; they provide an opportunity for you to come to peace with what was, and what is now.

Healing from Post-Traumatic Stress

> **Objectively, are you at fault for what happened to others? If so, how?**

_____

_____

_____

_____

_____

> **What could you have done (or not done) that would have helped the situation?**

_____

_____

_____

_____

_____

Forgiving Yourself

It is unlikely, but possible, that there was something that you could have done to change the outcome of the trauma. If that is the case, it is a difficult truth to live with. Nonetheless, feeling guilty about it now doesn't help. Maybe there is something you can do for the affected person or his or her family now. Frequently it is in giving to others that we receive the healing we need. I realize this may sound simplistic, but it is like spilling a glass of milk. You can't unspill it, but you can help wipe it up.

It is also important at this juncture that you find a way to forgive yourself. Carrying the burden of guilt only makes your life miserable—it doesn't fix what was. Many of us believe that to forgive is to forget, to make it as if the event never happened. Actually, to forgive means to acknowledge the wrong done and to choose not to carry that burden. In the case of a trauma, as in the spilt milk vignette, you cannot undo what was done or not done. But you can let it be in the past, make amends if necessary, and live a good life. One of my favorite writings on the topic is the chapter on forgiveness in *Women Who Run with the Wolves* by Clarissa Pinkola Estés. She delves into what forgiveness means in an eloquent, comprehensive manner.

There are many practices geared to facilitating forgiveness and letting go. Some are ceremonial or spiritual. For example, Carla had had an abortion forty years earlier and carried a lot of guilt about it. She understood that she had taken the only course of action that made sense to her at that time, but she still felt guilty. We created a ceremony in which she went out and bought baby booties, a pacifier, and a bib. Then we went into the woods, and as we buried those articles, she asked her image of the unborn child forgiveness for her actions. Afterward she reported that she still felt sad, but no longer guilty.

Maha felt guilty because she had been spared in a car accident that had claimed the lives of several of her friends. As a result it was hard for her to enjoy her life, always feeling that she didn't deserve it since others couldn't have it. She decided to go talk to her spiritual leader, who provided her with the perspective and guidance that she needed. She was then able to acknowledge that her lack of enjoyment didn't fix the situation and that her friends would not have wanted her to be miserable for the rest of her life.

Other practices are rational and pragmatic. For example, a client once saw a child being abused and felt that there was nothing he could do. He just stood there and did nothing, feeling terrible the whole while. For a long time the image haunted him and he felt very guilty about his lack of courage. He then decided to become a Big Brother to a couple of boys from violent families and feels that he is compensating and making a contribution. Frank felt terrible about not having been able to save his father, who fell and hemorrhaged to death. Even though he called 911, it was too late. Frank became a volunteer EMT and is now able to save other people's lives.

I invite you to contemplate what would make sense to you to help you let go of your guilt. Simply understanding that you did the best you could at the time might be sufficient. If not, I invite you to determine what endeavor would most suit your situation and personality. Ultimately, the form does not matter—it is the intention that is important. You might not be able to achieve self-forgiveness overnight, but over time you can release that burden from your psyche.

As you consider the topic of self-forgiveness, I invite you to ponder the following questions: How does feeling guilty serve you? How does your feeling guilty serve or help anyone else?

I hope that doing these exercises has alleviated your guilt, or has at least allowed you to revisit the circumstances of the trauma and your behavior at that time with greater clarity and perspective. Remember to make some time for yourself to transition back to your daily routine. Refer to Chapter 2 for self-care suggestions.

7

Dealing with Anxiety

Immediately after a trauma, or sometimes a little while later, once the immediate shock and numbness has worn off, many people find themselves feeling anxious. This is a normal, natural consequence of trauma and one of the key aspects of post-traumatic stress. Anxiety is a combination of thoughts, feelings, and physical sensations. It is a state of hyperarousal. Anxiety is frequently experienced as an overwhelming flood of distressing sensations that lead to feelings and thoughts that encroach on your everyday sense of well-being and on your usual activities. Sometimes these distressing thoughts and feelings can be directly traced back to aspects of the trauma, while at other times they seem to come out of nowhere and don't appear to make sense.

During and after a traumatic event, your whole system goes into survival preparedness: your adrenaline levels go up, your heartbeat speeds up, and you get ready to fight, flee, or freeze. (When we freeze, we look like nothing is happening, but our system is still in hyperarousal—which is not the same as action.) After a trauma, your system may not quite register that you are out of harm's way. It stays in preparedness. However, there is nothing to prepare for or against. So the "energy" of hyperarousal continues to float around in your body, sending messages to your brain that there is something wrong; we label this *anxiety*.

Anxiety can be free-floating—that is, present in some degree at all times—or can be a reaction triggered by some external stimulus such as a smell, touch, feel, sound, light, or darkness. These stimuli can also trigger a flashback (see Chapter 9), which can amplify the feeling of anxiety. After a traumatic experience, people often feel a slight, ever-present anxiety, which peaks to higher intensity during times of stress. For instance, anxiety can intensify when you are in circumstances similar to those of your trauma (like being stuck in the dark) or subsequent to a trigger (like a specific color or sensation).

There are many techniques for lessening anxiety that you can do on your own or with the help of others. Some people find using analytical techniques helpful in dealing with unsolicited intense emotions. Others find body-centered techniques more effective. Whatever seems more appropriate for you at any given time is what's best for you at that time. If you have used a specific approach in the past to help you in times of stress, you can always use that. In addition, you can explore some of the techniques in this chapter to add to your repertoire.

I suggest that you explore the various options available and discover what feels right for you. You will thus build a reservoir of techniques. You can then use the technique that feels most appropriate when circumstances warrant it. For example, you might choose to learn mind-calming techniques such as meditation or yoga, work with a psychotherapist, and/or find activities that are anxiety-reducing for you such as going for a walk, listening to music, writing, or one of the other activities suggested in Chapter 2.

Following is a list of symptoms usually associated with anxiety. Check off those that apply to you, and feel free to add any you experience that are not listed. Symptoms of anxiety range from the subtle to the obvious in their manifestation. They may include these:

Symptom	Have It	Had It
Relentless sense of fear	☐	☐
Sweating	☐	☐
Feeling cold	☐	☐
Having the jitters	☐	☐
Nervousness	☐	☐
Feeling wired	☐	☐
Rapid breathing	☐	☐
Having difficulty breathing	☐	☐
Rapid heartbeat	☐	☐
Tightening of the stomach	☐	☐

Healing from Post-Traumatic Stress

	Have It	Had It
Tightening of the throat	☐	☐
Having thoughts that go around and around	☐	☐
Feeling you can't move	☐	☐
Having irrational thoughts	☐	☐
Diarrhea	☐	☐
Headaches	☐	☐
Shaking	☐	☐
Tearing	☐	☐
Vomiting	☐	☐
Feeling stuck in a place	☐	☐
Feeling that a room is closing in on you	☐	☐
Not being able to think	☐	☐
Crying	☐	☐

Use the space below to add any other symptoms that are not listed here.

Symptom	Have It	Had It
_____	☐	☐
_____	☐	☐
_____	☐	☐
_____	☐	☐
_____	☐	☐

Reduce Anxiety with These Soothing Activities

Innumerable modalities of psychotherapy, mind-calming techniques, massage, and acupuncture, as well as other forms of body and energy work, have been found effective in reducing anxiety. Finding the right fit and the right practitioner for you is as important as the modality, if not more so. This is truly a case of all roads leading to Rome. So trust yourself to know what is right for you. Moreover, remember that what you need may change as you go through the process of healing and returning to personal normalcy. It may be beneficial to find new venues to assist you as you progress on your journey.

If your symptoms are mild, infrequent, and/or do not impinge on your everyday life, you might choose to just let it be and wait for them to subside. On the other hand, there is no need to be in any discomfort, so I encourage you to take whatever measures are available to assist you in healing. Furthermore, my experience is that if you tackle your discomforts when they are small, they don't get bigger and more difficult to eradicate later. If your symptoms are intense, frequent, or if they prevent you from functioning in your everyday life, I urge you to seek professional help. There are medicines and herbs to help with anxiety that you can obtain from a medical doctor or psychiatrist.

If you have dealt with anxiety in the past, by all means include those approaches that were previously beneficial to you. The following are some techniques that many people have found helpful in dealing with anxiety:

- Remember what you have done in the past that has helped relieve anxiety or stress. Write these techniques down; they are a helpful reference.
- Consciously remind yourself that this moment is *now* and not the same time and circumstance as that in which your trauma occurred. Eckart Tolle, a spiritual teacher, recommends that you let yourself know that in this very instant there is no problem. This might sound unrealistic or superficial, but I encourage you to try it. If you can keep yourself in the moment, things become easier to manage and fears seem to dissipate.
- Cross and uncross your fingers, alternating sides. Move your right thumb over your left thumb, your right pointer finger over your left pointer finger, your right middle finger over your left middle finger, and so on until you've moved all of the fingers on your right hand over the fingers on your left hand. Then do the same thing starting with moving your left thumb over your right thumb, and so on. Concentrate on becoming keenly aware of your hands and their movements. Notice the difference in one hand over the other. Feel the sensations of changing the finger positions. If you can, synchronize your breathing with each change of position.

- Physical activities, particularly strenuous ones, help reduce anxiety and release tension. Aerobic activities release body chemicals that are soothing and calming. You might find that playing a sport, running on the treadmill, going for a run, chopping wood, dancing, or doing any other physical activity of your choice will help alleviate your anxiety.
- Engage in an attention-demanding or engrossing project. Try working on an art project, cleaning your closets, or paying bills. When you focus on an activity that takes much of your attention, you can't think about something else, and therefore it is calming, for the moment at least. The more demanding the activity, the more of your attention it takes. For example, I take martial art classes. No matter what is going in my life, when I'm in class the only thing I can focus on is which foot to put where and what to do with my hands. I am still surprised that when I'm done with the class, whatever was bothering me before is not as intense.
- Focus your attention on the fact that you are anxious, and remind yourself that it will pass. You might say to yourself out loud or in your head something like, "I'm anxious, it feels lousy, *and* I know that I will not be anxious forever." Even if you don't quite believe it, give it a try!
- Recall a soothing time, event, or place. It has been proven that statements we make affect our brain waves and alter our sense of well-being. For example, think about being angry and notice what happens in your body. Now think about a lovely, wonderful time in your life and notice what happens. When you are feeling anxious, try thinking of a wonderful time, event, or place in your life. Create a soothing mental image. Be as clear as possible with the image, the feelings, the sensations, and the thoughts associated with that time, event, or place. Keep going back to it and remembering it until it is truly imprinted on your consciousness. Return to that image when you feel anxious.
- Become aware of all the times that you are *not* anxious. Note to yourself, *This moment I am feeling good, happy, or calm.* This awareness builds a foundation for your system to remember that you are not always anxious. You can then draw on that knowledge when you *are* feeling anxious.
- Concentrate on your breath. Count each individual breath so that you inhale on one, exhale on two, inhale on one, and so on. As an alternative, repeat the words "breathing in" and "breathing out" as you inhale

and exhale slowly. It is the focus on your breath that matters, not what you choose to say. If you are experiencing rapid breathing or panting, practice consciously slowing the breath down. Allow each breath to become a little deeper and a little longer until you can count to seven on the in breath and to seven on the out breath. Try to take big breaths that will go all the way down to fill up your belly.

■ Call or visit someone who helps you feel safe and comfortable.

Your Personal Soothing Activities

Use the space in this section to jot down activities that you know are soothing for you. When you've come up with two or three activities that seem good for you at this time, copy them on a piece of paper and stick it on your refrigerator, over your desk, or wherever you are likely to look when you are feeling anxious. Carry a copy in your wallet. You can also input them in your PalmPilot or use the list as a screen saver. It will serve as a reminder when you are in the midst of feeling anxious and you forget all about what you could do to help yourself. One of my clients has the word *safe* on her bathroom mirror and as a screen saver.

Activity: _____

_____

_____

Activity: _____

_____

_____

Activity: _____

_____

_____

Activity: _____

_____

_____

You might also want to review and revise the list periodically to make sure that the ideas you have there are still effective. You will find that different techniques work better at different times.

Stay in the Moment

Remember that your feeling of anxiety is just that—a *feeling* of anxiety. I invite you to do a reality check on whether any of these fears are valid in this very moment. What are the dangers of *this moment?* Are there dangers of this moment? Reminding yourself to stay in the moment might help you feel less anxious. It will also provide you with a new perspective and give you some distance between what you are feeling as a result of what happened in the past and what is happening in the moment.

You might feel as if these feelings of anxiety will last forever. They won't. It might take longer than you wish for the anxiety to dissipate, but if you are willing to be patient and kind toward yourself—the biggest ingredients in any change—and willing to take some steps toward your own healing, you will one day notice that you are feeling more like yourself again.

For example, Norman felt anxious most of the time, and his anxiety would peak whenever he saw any kind of police activity, particularly police barricades. He couldn't quite make sense of it until he remembered being in World War II as a young child and the terror that barricades had presented to him and his family. Although his anxiety did not fade completely, it only came up in specific circumstances, and because he understood where the feelings came from, he was able to work with them until they didn't last more than a few minutes.

Clarissa would feel anxious in the subway after having been stuck there during a power failure. Over time her symptoms completely disappeared. She reported she had been stuck in the subway, read her book, and only later realized that she used to be anxious in that circumstance.

The following exercise is intended to help you focus on what makes you anxious and what you can do about it. As you go through it, you might review the suggestions in this chapter for reducing anxiety . I also encourage you to add any activity that has helped you deal with anxiety in the past.

What Makes Me Anxious	**What Might Help**
_____	_____
_____	_____
_____	_____
_____	_____
_____	_____
_____	_____

Whatever anxiety you are feeling now can and will abate with time and a willingness on your part to do the emotional work that is required for healing. By doing the exercises in this book, you are already taking a step in the right direction—you do not have to be anxious forever!

I hope that going over this material reassured you that your feelings are a perfectly normal and natural reaction to trauma. At the same time, going through these exercises can be unsettling and anxiety-producing. Therefore, before you go on to your daily activities, take time to transition. Do something loving, fun, or soothing until you feel ready to return to your everyday life.

8

Grief

It is normal to feel loss and grief when a part of your life, and what you once took for granted, has been altered. Grief is a feeling that includes sadness, pain, hurt, and sometimes anger or resentment. It is often present in the aftermath of a trauma because most traumas involve loss: loss of a loved one, loss of an illusion or belief, loss of a part of one's physical body, loss of material things. Grief is a natural and healthy reaction to loss. Frequently, grief (possibly combined with anger, relief, guilt, or gratitude) is also felt by those close to you, sometimes because your trauma has a direct impact on them, sometimes because it reminds them of a similar personal situation. Not everyone who has gone through a trauma feels grief, however. You may have gone through your trauma with very few or no losses, and you might be feeling more gratitude than anything else.

Grief is seldom given its due time in our culture. We are supposed to feel it and "get over it." Yet grief can last a long time, particularly if it is not allowed full expression. Unexpressed and unaddressed grief can turn into depression or manifest itself physiologically as ailments. As previously stated, ancient wisdom, as well as my experience, indicates that it takes at least four seasons for an individual to go through the stages of grief.

Bethany is a highly competent, intelligent career woman. Her mother died after a short but intense bout with esophageal cancer. Bethany and her family were bereft. A month or so after Bethany's mother's death, she came into my office and burst into tears because she had to go clothes shopping and her mother would not be with her. She felt that she couldn't pick out clothes herself. She missed her mother terribly. She thought of her mother every day and didn't think it would ever be better. She felt that she had no one to go to for advice. She reviewed the last few months of her mother's life. Maybe she should have done more, or something different to keep her mother alive. She was grateful that she had taken the time to spend with her mother before her death, so there was no guilt, just sadness and grief.

The first holidays felt torturous. Her mother had organized and hosted all the holidays. Who would do it? Where would it be? We talked about the need to create new rituals that honored her mother but also represented the family's new situation. Bethany, her siblings, and their father decided that they would first go to the cemetery and then have dinner at their parents' home, with each sibling bringing some of the food. Every holiday that year had to be reinvented—created anew to accommodate the loss while embracing the new. After each one, she would say to me, "Well, we made it through this one."

Over time, the sharpness of Bethany's grief diminished as she worked through the grieving process, honored her mother's memory, and adjusted her life to the loss. Bethany reported that she didn't think about her mother every minute of every day as she had at first. One week she came in and said, "I feel a bit guilty—I actually didn't think about my mother at all this week, until I walked in here." Now, two years later, Bethany's life has returned to a new normalcy. Bethany still misses her mother periodically, but it is not a constant sharp pain.

> Grief is a natural emotion that arises as a result of loss. Nonetheless, if you have been feeling intense grief for quite a while, if your grief is impeding your daily life, or if you feel unable to get out of it, it is time to seek counseling. You can choose a mental health provider, a support group, or some other form of support. Also, certain medications can help get you over the hump. Please be good to yourself and avail yourself of existing resources.

This chapter invites you to look at your grief. The goal of this process is not to take away your grief, or even to lessen it—only time will do that. Its aim is to guide you in validating and honoring your feelings and to give you an opportunity to recognize that grief, in all its aspects, is a normal and natural consequence of having experienced a trauma. This chapter also offers you an opportunity to look at the grief that might be felt by those close to you: your family, friends, or coworkers. Doing so might help you better understand their attitude and behavior toward you.

Before you do the following exercises, make sure that you give yourself enough time, a quiet space, a box of tissues, and whatever you need for safety and personal comfort. Following are some of the reasons you might be feeling grief:

- Loss of a loved one
- Loss of a part of your body
- Loss of a mental faculty
- Loss of a belief or idea (for example, the belief that you are safe)
- Loss of property
- Loss of work
- Loss of financial security

☞ *Write, draw, and/or make a collage of your losses. Some might be big, others small. Do not judge them. They all matter.*

Healing from Post-Traumatic Stress

Acknowledging Sorrow and Resentment

Sadness or sorrow is the underpinning of grief. It is that emotion that brings tears to our eyes, constriction or pain in our heart. Sorrow is a longing for that which is not—sometimes for what was and no longer is, sometimes for what was not and now can never be.

Barbara lost her husband in an accident. Although there was a lot of love between them, and they loved many of the same things, their relationship of late had not been the best. She had in fact been debating whether to take a leave from the relationship because it had become too difficult. When her husband died in a car accident, Barbara was very sad. She missed him—his conversation, his wit, his optimism. She was sad that the relationship had become sour in the last few years, and she sorrowed that now it was too late, that they would never be reconciled, there was no more chance.

During our times together, we talked about her husband, what it had been like living with him, the good things, and the not-so-good things. We created rituals to let go of the bad stuff and to embrace the goodness that had been there. We honored the grief and the loss, and we rejoiced at the freedom that was letting her become truer to herself. After a couple of years, Barbara found a new partner. Her comment is, "I don't have what I had, but I didn't have what I have now."

In the space below, write, draw, and/or make a collage of the things that you feel sad about.

Healing from Post-Traumatic Stress

Sometimes grief can have elements of anger or resentment. Kevin was badly injured at his job. As a result he had to go on total disability. He had loved what he did and felt proud of his skills. And here he was, feeling useless, in pain a lot of the time, not knowing what to do with himself. He couldn't fall back on his favorite distractions, which were high-impact activities like hiking and mountain climbing. He couldn't even ride his bicycle.

Kevin felt that he had lost his complete identity, his whole sense of self, and he was angry—angry that he was in pain, angry that he couldn't work, angry that he couldn't do his sport activities. He felt that his life was over, and he felt sad for the things he would never be able to do again, sad that he wouldn't be able to show his children the beauty of the outdoors as he had loved it. He even felt sad and sometimes angry at the way his wife looked at him with such compassion.

Here is the good news: Kevin became very involved in his physical recovery. He discovered gentle yoga and long quiet walks, which he shares with his children. And the best part is that he accidentally discovered an ability to make sculptures out of things. He now has a fulfilling life, though not the one he had planned. Occasionally he feels wistful for the past, but overall, he loves his new life.

The key was that before he could get through his grief, he had to acknowledge all its facets—the sorrow and the resentment. That gave him the clarity to proceed on to a new way of being. The following exercise invites you to look at those aspects of your grief. Like any other feelings and thoughts, they are not bad or good. They just are, and by becoming aware of them, you move forward into the possibility of a new sense of well-being.

Write, draw, and/or make a collage of those things that you feel angry or resentful about.

Healing from Post-Traumatic Stress

Sometimes it is hard after going through a traumatic event to understand that other people are also dealing with their own feelings about the event—and sometimes about you. The following exercises aim to clarify the reasons for people's feelings and their behavior toward you.

Stan, a fifteen-year-old basketball player, lost a part of two of his left-hand fingers while playing with a firecracker bomb. He was upset and angry, but surprisingly to him, not too badly so. He had other interests and somehow was able to put the incident into a healthy perspective. His family, on the other hand, was in an upheaval about it. His father was furious, and his mother and sister wailed and were overprotective and overbearing. Stan couldn't stand it. He loved his family, but just wanted out.

As we explored the reactions of Stan's family, we discovered an explanation for their reactions. Stan's father worked as a carpenter, like his father and grandfather before him. He couldn't imagine that his son would do anything different, and he felt that this injury would prevent him from being able to work. (Meanwhile Stan, who was good at math, wanted to be an accountant.) Stan's father was scared about his son's future but didn't know how to express it properly, so he reacted with anger.

Stan's mother wanted to take care of him and make sure that something like this—or any other misfortune—wouldn't happen again, and so she overdid her caretaking. Once Stan understood what was going on, he was able to talk to each person in his family and explain that he was not an invalid, but that he needed to learn to take care of himself in a new way.

Of course they were sad that this had happened. Over time, Stan's fingers healed and he learned to use his hand efficiently. This incident, though unfortunate, helped the family understand each other better. And Stan feels good about himself that he made it through, navigated the medical establishment, the rehabilitation process, the emotional roller coaster. He said, "You know, I think I can handle anything life deals me."

People close to you (or not so close to you) may be feeling grief as well. If you are lucky, you can have an open conversation about how your trauma has affected them; you can share thoughts and feelings and deepen your relationship. Unfortunately, in our culture it is often not so easy to talk to others about their thoughts and feelings; even in families many topics are taboo. So that leaves you doing guesswork. Sometimes you know why the person is feeling grief because you know his or her history or because you know that they are close to you and, like Stan's parents, are worried about you.

The following exercise is intended to help you understand other people's reactions and help you cope with them. Jot down what you think their grief might be about.

Person   **Why the Person Is Feeling Grief**

_____   _____

_____   _____

_____   _____

_____   _____

People have many different ways of expressing emotions—particularly the difficult ones such as hurt, fear, grief, and anger. In this exercise, I invite you to ponder how the people in your life are relating to you because of the grief that they are feeling as a result of your trauma. In Stan's example, his father could not express his worry and his grief, so he became furious and acted angrily.

                                              How Grief Affects How the Person
Person   **Relates to You**

_____   _____

_____   _____

_____   _____

_____   _____

I hope that the information you have gathered helps you make sense of other people's reactions toward you and makes you feel better if you are not receiving the support that you wish you would get.

Expressing Your Grief

Working through grief and all its aspects takes time and needs expression. It is important that you give yourself the time and space to grieve in the many ways that you need to do it. The list below provides some ideas of what you might want to do to express your feelings:

- **Rail, scream, punch, kick, or stomp.** Make sure you do it in a safe way so that you do not hurt yourself, anyone else, or any property. One of my favorite expressions of anger was given to me by a teacher. Get a metal pan and a wooden spoon. Bang the spoon on the pan as hard as you can and scream all the things that you are angry or resentful about. I also like to set an alarm to contain the amount of time. Usually ten minutes is plenty.
- **Write in stream of consciousness.** Write whatever comes to your mind without worrying about sequence, grammar, or spelling. You can pour out your sadness, your anger, your hurt, or whatever is weighing on your heart and mind into the writing. You can then keep it or tear it up or burn it.
- **Sing or compose a song.** Like the writing, you can keep it, or not.
- **Dance or move.** Running, walking, and other aerobic activities are good as well. However, movement and dance are less structured than other forms of movement. There is a more spontaneous flow, especially if you can allow your body to move you rather than trying to choreograph something. Remember that in this type of moving, being still is considered movement.
- **Light a candle.** In many traditions, candles are used to connect to oneself to the divine. In some, the candle's flame is symbolic of purification; in others, the flame is symbolic of fire and wind, which are the elements that help us get rid of unwanted energy. Flames are also a wonderful point of focus. Watching a fire can be mesmerizing and often soothing. You can light a candle and imagine that the flame is burning off your grief, your sorrow, your hurt; that its light is coming into your body, lighting up all the dark places; or that the light at the end of the tunnel is close at hand.

These are just a few ways that you can express your grief—there are many other actions and activities that will help to alleviate your feelings as well. Take some time to jot down any other activities you can think of that have helped you to feel better in the past. You might also want to keep this list handy so you can refer to it easily when you need it.

Activity: _____

_____

_____

Activity: _____

_____

_____

Activity: _____

_____

_____

Activity: _____

_____

_____

Contemplating your grief may have left you feeling heavy and down. Take some time to honor those feelings, then do whatever feels nurturing to you to transition back into your everyday life. Remember that, just like the seasons, your feelings will change.

9

Flashbacks, Dreams, and Nightmares

Although dreams, daydreams, and flashbacks are a common experience in most people's lives, their content, quality, and frequency seem to change after a trauma. How that manifests itself is different for each person. You may find yourself remembering more of your dreams; you may find yourself remembering less. You may have had a rich dream life that has dried up. You may now find yourself remembering dreams or daydreams when you didn't before.

Immediately after your traumatic incident you may feel that you are constantly reliving it. The experience of reliving an event as if it were happening in the moment is called a flashback. Some people don't have flashbacks, and some have them much later in their healing process. The same is true of daydreams, which differ from flashbacks in the intensity and exactitude of the experience. Remember that you are a unique individual with an inimitable process. Honor your own process.

Dreams

There is a multitude of theories about dreams, where they come from and what they mean. Freud called dreams "the royal road to the unconscious." He believed that thoughts, ideas, and feelings that could not be expressed in waking life were revealed through dreams and that dreams were a means to understand the patient's neuroses. Jung believed that dreams were a gateway to the "collective unconscious," that through dreams we can access information and knowledge that is universal to all human beings. Many indigenous cultures believe that dreams are a way to communicate with spirits and other beings that do not live on this earth plane. For some, the "dreamtime" is a parallel reality to that of the waking time. Other cultures believe that there are different types of dreams: teaching dreams, in which we are taught something that will be useful in our waking life; prediction dreams that let us know ahead of time what will happen; and incorporation dreams in which we are given the opportunity to work through events of our everyday life.

To better understand your dreams, it is helpful to have a basic understanding of sleep. There are different stages of sleep. It is believed that whether or not we remember our dreams, we all dream in what is called REM sleep. Each person has his or her own dream experience and relationship to his or her dreams. Some people dream in everyday images, others in wild phantasmagoric images, others in movie form, and others yet in metaphors or symbolic characters. Dreams can be pleasant, soothing, or even healing. Scary and upsetting dreams are generally referred to as nightmares. Some dreams are highly charged emotionally, others are devoid of feelings, like watching a movie from afar.

Remembering dreams may also be periodic. You may find yourself remembering your dreams actively for a while, then not remembering, then remembering again. As with what dreams are all about, there doesn't seem to be any universal explanation for this. Whether or not you remember your dreams, and what kind of dream life you have, in no way determines the state of your mental health.

Nightmares

Nightmares are frightening or upsetting dreams, usually of high emotional intensity. Like dreams, they may be representational of everyday events, or they may have highly imaginative or sci-fi elements. What matters is the feeling associated with the material. Again, having or not having nightmares is in no way indicative of your healing progress.

Daydreams

Daydreams happen when you are awake, but your attention is not focused in the present moment. You may be sitting reading a book, while your attention may actually be on your grocery list, the vacation that you just took, or the movie that you are about to go see. You may also be fantasizing about an event that is going to happen, or that you wish would happen. You may be quite aware of your daydreams, or you may just suddenly notice that you've "spaced out" or that you haven't been paying attention to what you are doing, like taking a trip and not quite remembering how you got from point A to point B.

After a trauma you might find yourself "spacing out" more, thinking about what happened, what you did or didn't do, or what you wish you had or hadn't done. You might possibly replay the event but change the circumstances or outcome. One of my clients who had been raped would replay the scene, but in her daydream, she would hit the rapist over the head, run away, and find a safe haven.

The quality of daydreaming is also present in the hypnagogic state, those few seconds or minutes before you are fully asleep or before you are fully awake, that ephemeral time that straddles sleep time and awake time.

Flashbacks

Flashbacks can occur while you are fully awake and aware, as a daydream, or in dream time as a nightmare. A flashback is characterized by fully reexperiencing the event that you are remembering. It is as if you are living the incident in the moment or you were transported back in time to the actual event that occurred however long ago. You have the same images, thoughts, feelings, and often the same bodily sensations that you had at the time of the incident.

Flashbacks can come unbidden for no apparent reason at all, or may be triggered by a sight, a sound, a smell, a word, or a song. For example, a client who had been across the street when the World Trade Center towers were hit by the airplanes would relive the whole scene whenever she heard any sound resembling an airplane. Another person, who had escaped from a fire, would have flashbacks when he heard a certain song that had played on the radio at the time of that fire.

How to Work with Your Dreams, Nightmares, Daydreams, and Flashbacks

There are many techniques that can help you work with these aftereffects of trauma. The following processes allow you to use your awareness to reduce the negative impact of unpleasant or scary nightmares, daydreams, or flashbacks. They are some of the techniques that my clients have found helpful. There are also many others that are equally beneficial.

Dreams and Nightmares

It seems that since the beginning of civilization, humans have wanted to know about their dreams. Because of this eternal fascination with dreams, we've developed many ideas about what dreams mean and how to cull that meaning. I would like to present three modern methods of looking at dreams. You can use all of them, one of them, or none of them. You might already have your own way of working with dreams. If that is the case, I encourage you to use that.

Explore your dreams when you are awake. The goal of this technique is to achieve a greater understanding of the meaning of your dream. All of the aspects of your dream can tell you something, regardless of what they are. For example, a chair may have as much information as a person. As you go over your dream, notice which element in your dream seems most salient or calls for your attention. Then begin a dialogue with that element, asking it what it is trying to show you.

For example, let's say that you dreamed you went into a department store and were drawn to the food counter. Focus your attention on the food counter. What does it look like? What foods are there? Does any one item draw your attention? What does it remind you of? What is it trying to show you? Then move on to the next most conspicuous aspect of the dream and repeat the process until you feel satisfied. Usually working with one or two aspects of the dream is quite enough information.

Write down your dreams. Another technique that many people find helpful is to write down your dream as you awake. You can write it down later on in the day as well, though this is not considered as effective. Write down as much of the dream as you remember, and make sure to include the feelings that you had during the dream and as you awoke. If you don't remember the details of the dream, concentrate on your feelings.

When you're done writing, take a few minutes to write down any associations that come to mind from the dream. Include any thoughts, feelings, or memories that come up. In addition to providing you with insight into the dream, this technique also provides an outlet for the thoughts and feelings of the dream so you don't have to carry them throughout the day.

Lucid dreaming. This last technique is one method of working with dreams while still in the dream. The underpinning belief for this technique is that we are the authors of our dreams and that therefore we have the ability to redirect and change them while in the dream. The process of lucid dreaming allows you to influence the dream while in the dream state by giving yourselves directives prior to going to sleep. There are many excellent books on the topic. In a very simplified form, this is how it works.

Before you go to sleep, remind yourself that you are the author of your dream and that you have the ability to change or impact what is happening. Then, while in the dream, give yourself directions such as "This is a dream. I have a choice of what is going to happen next, and this is how I want it to change." Or you can remind yourself that you are in a dream and that it is not real life. Or you can let yourself watch what is happening as if it were a movie. If the dream is really disturbing to you, you can use lucid dreaming to end the dream by telling yourself, "I know this is a dream, and I want it to stop. Now!"

While this technique might sound implausible at first, with practice, it can work for many people. You can become more of an observer of your dreams. As a result the fierceness and terror of nightmares have less impact on your psyche. One of my clients basically rid herself of her nightmares by telling the images and thoughts in the nightmare to go away. Through lucid dreaming she was able to control her dreams so that she focused on pleasant images.

You can also use lucid dreaming to change the outcome or events of your dream. Use your imagination. If you are in a flood, get a boat; if you are in a fire, get a hose; if you are in battle, get a shield; if you are in a plane, get a parachute. You get the idea. A young client of mine who had been traumatized by being molested used to have a terrible recurrent nightmare that a pair of glowing red eyes came through her window and were going to get her. In the dream she was terrified and immobilized. After we worked together, she came up with the solution of having Pac-Man (a video-game cartoon character that ate others) come to gobble up the eyes. She practiced in awake time. Then she practiced setting the intention and in her mind asking Pac-Man to protect her during her sleep. Shortly after that she was able to visualize Pac-Man in her dreams when the eyes came. After a few weeks the eyes—and their terrifying impact—were completely gone.

The same approach does not work for everyone or every time. I invite you to think about what might be helpful to you while you are awake, then experiment in dream time to see what works for you. You may not succeed right away; like all new practices it may take a few times to master the techniques.

Daydreams and Flashbacks

Although daydreams and flashbacks are similar, they are not quite the same. As mentioned earlier, flashbacks have the same content and intensity as the original event, while daydreams may feel somewhat more removed. Both daydreams and flashbacks remove you from the awareness of the present moment. I once missed my train stop because I was so intent in remembering a vacation I had taken a few years back and wishing I were back there (actually, in my head, I was back there!).

When you are having a disturbing daydream or flashback, it helps to become aware that you are daydreaming or having a flashback and consciously bring your attention back to the present moment. You can do that by consciously noticing where you are, who is around you, and what is going on. Notice the sounds and pay attention to any sensation in your body. A good technique is to find five things about the place you are in that you like and five things that you dislike. Once you have done that, remind yourself that you were in the midst of a daydream or flashback and that everything is okay in the present here-and-now. If you feel scared, frazzled, and shaken up by your daydreams and flashbacks, refer to Chapter 7 for suggestions on how to calm yourself.

Remember that all of these techniques are simplified and not meant to take the place of in-depth dream work. If you are having a difficult time with nightmares and flashbacks, or with sleep in general, it would be a good idea to seek some professional help.

Your Dream Journal

The following pages are provided for you to record your dreams, nightmares, daydreams, and flashbacks. You might want to just write them down, or you might want to explore what they represent to you and what you might do to make them less bothersome. If you would like to record your dreams over a period of time, it might be a good idea for you to start a dream journal. As with all the material suggested in this manuscript, it is important that you remember that whatever you put on paper is private, "for your eyes only."

🖋 *Write, draw, and/or make a collage of your dreams or nightmares.*

✐ Write, draw, and/or make a collage of your daydreams or flashbacks.

Flashbacks, Dreams, and Nightmares

Use this space to express any insights about your dreams, nightmares, day-dreams, and flashbacks.

Take some time to think about what you think might be helpful for you in dealing with your unpleasant dreams, nightmares, daydreams, or flashbacks. I have presented some techniques that you might find helpful, but these are not the only options. Use this space to record any other techniques that work for you:

_____

_____

_____

_____

_____

Doing the preceding exercises might have felt comforting or distressing. You may feel good that you now have tools to work with your dreams, nightmares, daydreams, and flashbacks, or you may feel rattled by remembering them.

If you are feeling a bit raw and shaken, make sure to take your time before you go on to your everyday activities. If you feel at a loss as to what to do at this moment to take care of yourself, you might want to refer to Chapter 2 for ideas.

10

The Ripple Effect

There's a Buddhist teaching that every action and every event of our lives is like a pebble dropped in a pond. Its ripples affect the whole pond, and the shore it touches, and the vegetation that grows in it, and the animals that live in and around it, and . . . You get the picture. Small pebbles create small ripples; big stones create large ripples. Each ripple creates ripples that intersect with other ripples and create new ripples. A traumatic event is like a large stone. It creates lots of ripples. Some of the ripples are directly about dealing with and recovering from the trauma, others are more distant and seemingly unrelated.

This chapter looks at the ripples that a traumatic event can create in your life. These ripples touch, among others, your work, your relationships, your way of being in the world, your values, your aspirations, and your dreams. Times of immediate danger and turmoil propel us into action—into doing what needs to happen in the moment, whether it is fight, flight, or freeze—without much thought about anything else. The aftermath, on the other hand, oftentimes harbingers reassessment. As discussed in the previous chapters, it is common to have thoughts about whether you did the right thing, or could have done anything differently.

In the aftermath of trauma, some people find themselves pondering philosophical questions such as, *What is my life about? Am I devoting my time to the things that matter to me?* Some of the comments that I heard many times after the attack on the World Trade Center were, "Do I want to be working this hard?" and "No one on their deathbed ever said they wish they had worked more." Many people also expressed sentiments along the lines of "Maybe I should realign my priorities," "I always wanted to learn to dance," "Maybe it's time I went back to school," "I want to spend more quality time with my family," "I want to reconnect with my spiritual practice," or "I want to start that hobby."

After a major event, whether positive or negative, such as the birth of a child, a marriage, a graduation, a death, an illness, a promotion, losing a job, or moving, it is normal and natural to review your life and reassess what is important to you. Trauma is a major life event; it is common afterward for people to want to make changes in their lives and reevaluate their priorities.

A note of caution: Do not take any precipitous, impulsive action. Whatever reassessment or decision you come up with, give yourself some time—a few months at least—before you implement it. Give yourself the time to think through the pros and cons of what you would like to do before making any major changes in your life. The only exception to this rule is if you are in an abusive or life-threatening situation (such as if a family member is mistreating you or your children or if you are in an area that is not safe because of a natural disaster like a flood, an earthquake, or a tornado). In those cases, leave the situation as soon as possible. Find a relative or friend to stay with, call the National Domestic Violence Hotline at 800-799-SAFE or the Red Cross, or go to your local city hall or hospital.

Here are two scenarios that exemplify two ways to go about making a major life change, at the opposite ends of the spectrum.

The first was impulsive, and this type of change is not recommended. Arlet's house was burglarized. She decided that her life wasn't working and that this was the last straw. She impulsively left her marriage, her job, and her hometown. She did not examine the reasons for her unhappiness and did not give much thought to what her options were. As she said to me, "I just want out!" A few months later she found herself repeating the same behaviors and relationships and being as unhappy as she had prior to the traumatic incident. So she moved again, got another job, another relationship. That didn't work either. The good news is that, after that, Arlet noticed that she was repeating the same patterns. Last I heard, a few years ago, she was in recovery and therapy and had decided to start looking at what it was that really made her so miserable. I've not heard from her since, and I hope that she is doing well.

The second example is a man I know who took some time to reevaluate what was important to him. Marcus had been working on Wall Street since he graduated college. He wanted to be an artist, but in his family of high-powered professionals, he felt that would not be allowed. No one had ever said so to him, but he felt that there was an expectation that he should follow the lineage. So he did all the right things. He got married, had children, and lived in the suburbs. Marcus had a good life. He loved his wife and children, but he felt that there was an emptiness that he could not describe.

After 9/11 the feeling of "What am I doing with my life?" became stronger. We explored what he would do if he could do anything he wanted. He said he had always loved doing things with his hands and was good at it. He thought sculpting and furniture making would be fun and satisfying. But he didn't know if he would be good at it or how to make enough money to support his family.

He took some sculpting classes and found out that yes, he was good at it and loved it. He decided that what he wanted to do was go live in a small town and make a living from his sculpting and furniture making. Fortunately, his wife was willing to make the move. She could do her work practically anywhere. The children were young enough that a move would not have a negative impact on them.

After some searching, they found a place where there was a small but thriving artist colony, and they decided to move there. The last I heard, Marcus was happy sculpting, making rustic furniture, and working for a retail chain part-time to help with the bills. His wife continues her high-income work, and they have changed their lifestyle. It took them a little over a year to make the shift, and then another couple of years to adjust to the change. As I was writing this chapter, I received a postcard announcing a show and sale of Marcus's work.

Of course, both of these are instances of extreme change. Most changes people make are more in the middle range. This may be the time for you to see a career counselor, go back to school, seek counseling to work through your feelings, or explore other places to live. Having said that, I want to encourage you again to take your time. Think about what it is that you want to change and what you want the new situation to provide you with. Explore your options and do some research. Determine if, and how, the new situation you are considering will accomplish what you want. Even if you feel uncomfortable or unhappy in your current situation, a few months of exploration and planning will make a positive difference in the long run—again, unless it is a dangerous, abusive situation, in which case you need to change your situation as soon as possible.

The following pages are designed as a guide for you to explore the areas of your life that might have been touched, or rattled, by the trauma you went through. Some of the questions may not be relevant to your situation—just skip them and move on to the next question. These exercises are meant to bring out both the positive and the negative aspects of your present life and lifestyle and to provide a guideline to examine those areas of your life that might have been affected by the trauma. The themes I invite you to ponder are relationships, work, place of residence, and personal interests.

As with the other exercises in this book, you can write, draw, or make a collage of your answers. You can also, of course, use some other modality that suits you better, such as sculpting, model making, or any tangible form that will concretely express your thoughts and feelings. Make sure you have enough quiet time to contemplate the questions, to reflect, to dream, and to consider. There is a lot of material in this chapter, and trying to cover it all at once might be overwhelming. My suggestion is that you take each theme independently, maybe even on separate occasions. If you find that you are having a particularly hard time with a section, take a break and come back to it at a later time. There is no rush, no deadline. If you find that these questions point to areas in your life that are stressful, difficult, or affect your quality of life, contact a therapist, a counselor, a cleric, or someone you trust who can be loving, nonjudgmental, and wise to help you.

Personal Relationships

Most of us are involved in many different kinds of relationships, from the most casual to the most intimate and everything in between. Of course, the more intimate the relationship—whether with a partner, a parent, a child, or a best friend—the more likely it is that that relationship will be impacted by the events of our lives. Trauma can affect relationships. Sometimes for the better: we become closer, more connected, more intimate. We recognize the gifts from that person that we had not paid attention to or had taken for granted. Sometimes for the worse: we become more distant, less compatible; everything about the other person annoys us; we wonder what we saw in that person in the first place, and sometimes it is a wake-up call as to the imbalance or destructiveness of that particular relationship.

In this exercise you are invited to focus on your relationships. Your thoughts and feelings about each of the following relationships may have changed since your trauma. Simply notice what those changes are. You don't have to do anything about them, although you might choose to.

Use the following space to express how each of these relationships has been affected.

Parents

_____
_____
_____
_____
_____
_____
_____

Siblings

_____
_____
_____
_____
_____
_____
_____

Partner

_____
_____
_____
_____

The Ripple Effect

_____
_____
_____

Children

_____
_____
_____
_____
_____

Other Relatives

_____
_____
_____
_____
_____

Friends

_____
_____
_____
_____
_____
_____

Coworkers

_____
_____
_____

Healing from Post-Traumatic Stress

_____

_____

_____

Acquaintances

_____

_____

_____

_____

_____

_____

_____

Others

_____

_____

_____

_____

_____

_____

_____

Sometimes after a traumatic experience, we notice certain things about other people that either we didn't notice before or that didn't bother us then, but annoy us now. Or sometimes we want more or different things from a certain relationship than we did before the trauma. We don't want the relationship to evaporate, but we need it to change in order to be able to maintain it. The following exercise provides you with a concrete means of setting down what changes need to happen in which relationships.

After her third miscarriage, Vasant was devastated. She so wanted children. She became depressed and despondent. It was hard for her to be interested in anything. She felt as if she was walking through life without being here. She grieved the loss of her unborn babies, she grieved the loss of the life she had wanted, and she was angry that life was treating her badly. She called on Anna, her "best friend" from childhood, for support. Vasant had always been there for Anna through her trials and difficulties. Vasant's other friends had always told her that Anna was not a good friend, but Vasant always defended her. Now Vasant realized that Anna was not there for her, that she was not available for support and wasn't interested in going out of her way to help Vasant. Vasant spoke to Anna about her disappointment, but although Anna said she understood, her behavior did not change and she continued to put her own desires first. It made Vasant very sad, but after a while she began to realize how unbalanced the relationship had been all these years. She realized that although she had believed that she needed Anna for support and as an entrée to other friendships, it was actually the other way around. Vasant had lots of friends who cared about her and were there for her. She became closer to those people, and although she continues her relationship with Anna, it is much more superficial and distant.

On the other hand, Juliana and her husband had been married for forty-some years when she was diagnosed with breast cancer. It was relatively minor. The doctors were able to remove the entire tumor easily, and after six months of further treatment Juliana was given a clean bill of health. Nonetheless, the episode shook her to the core. She realized that she lived her life for others (mostly her family), not herself, and she wanted to have more of her own life. Her children were grown, so that was not much of an issue, but she had to redefine her relationship with her husband and her older sister, both of whom she realized depended too much on her. She hadn't quite noticed how much before. It was not easy for her to start saying, "No, I don't want to do this" or "I want to do this," even when her husband was not happy about it, and it was difficult for him to have to accommodate to her wants and her scheduling. But they were able to talk it through and slowly come to new "house rules" that in the end gave both of them greater freedom, brought them closer, and enabled them to have more fun together.

In which of your relationships would you like to create change? What are those changes? Are there changes that you need to make, are there changes that you need the other person to make, or both?

Relationship	Change

_____ _____
_____ _____
_____ _____
_____ _____

✎ *What needs to occur to make those changes possible?*

_____
_____
_____
_____
_____

✎ *How can you make that happen?*

_____
_____
_____
_____
_____

Trauma and its aftermath often provide us with an opportunity to reevaluate our life and our relationships. This may be an opportunity for you to bring closure to some of your relationships or say things that you haven't. You may want to tell someone that you love and appreciate him or her; you might want to let someone know that he or she hurt you or that you are holding anger toward him or her.

Paul's father had a sudden massive stroke on both sides of the brain. The doctors did not know whether he would ever regain any of his faculties. Paul's sister Devika lived far away and had not spoken to her father in years. However, at Paul's urging she came to see their father. By the time Devika arrived to see her father he had already recovered substantially, better than any of the doctors had hoped for. At first it was very awkward. However, Devika was able to talk with her dad, and they were able to forgive each other for the hurt that they had caused each other. For the first time in years they are able to be together as a family. The father is doing better and better, and they are now looking forward to spending the next holiday all together.

So, as you think about the people you listed, is there anything that you'd like to say to any one of them (or to others not mentioned) that somehow you have never gotten around to saying? This might be the right time to do so. You can speak to the person directly, or if that feels too threatening or difficult, you can write a letter, send a card, or even an e-mail. There is a Native American saying, "Today is a good day to die." It is meant to remind us that we should live each day well, as if were our last. Having no unfinished business with the people in your life is one of the ways to live well and to bring joy into your life.

Make a list of those people to whom you'd like to say something and what you would like to say to them. If you need more room, feel free to take a large pad of paper and use a page for each person to answer the questions below.

Person's name: _____

What would you like to say to that person? _____
_____
_____

How would you want to communicate? _____
_____
_____

What stops you? _____
_____
_____

What would make it feasible for you to contact that person? _____
_____
_____
_____

What do you think would happen if you communicated with that person?
_____
_____
_____

Person's name: _____

What would you like to say to that person? _____
_____
_____

How would you want to communicate? _____
_____
_____

What stops you? _____
_____
_____

What would make it feasible for you to contact that person? _____
_____
_____

What do you think would happen if you communicated with that person?
_____
_____
_____

Person's name: _____

What would you like to say to that person? _____
_____
_____

How would you want to communicate? _____
_____
_____

What stops you? _____
_____
_____

What would make it feasible for you to contact that person? _____
_____
_____

What do you think would happen if you communicated with that person?
_____
_____

Reviewing this exercise may propel you to take the opportunity to heal some relationships. Take note of those people whom you would like to contact and how you would like to do that, and then do it. It might be big, as in the vignette about Devika and her father, or relatively simple as with Juliana and her family. It may also be a chance to let go of relationships that are not healthy for you, like the relationship between Vasant and Anna.

Bravo! You've just completed a huge piece of work. It is arduous for anyone to scrutinize his or her relationships. It takes courage and commitment. Some of what you discovered may have felt reassuring. On the other hand, some old wounds may have gotten scratched open. Please make some time to take care of yourself in whatever way feels good for you at this time.

Work

Like Marcus, many of us do our job without too much thought about it. It's what we do. We don't hate it, we don't love it, we just do it. Of course, some of us love our work. It nurtures us, excites us, makes us feel good about ourselves and the product we generate (whether it is concrete or a service), and it enhances our lives. If you are one of those lucky people who love what they do, you might skip this exercise. You might instead spend a little time noting what about your work life makes you feel good enough to express gratitude about it.

As mentioned earlier, a traumatic event can shake up all the aspects of our lives, including the way we view our work life. The following exercises present you with questions to help you clarify your relationship to your work by assessing how you regarded your work prior to your trauma, how you feel about it now, and what changes, if any, you would like to implement.

How did you feel about your work prior to your trauma?

_____

_____

_____

_____

_____

_____

How do you feel about your work now?

_____

_____

_____

> **If your feelings have changed, how have they altered?**

_____

_____

_____

_____

> **Is this a positive change? If so, how?**

_____

_____

_____

_____

> **Is this a negative change? If so, how?**

_____

_____

_____

_____

> 🍃 **If the change is a negative one, you might be able to do something about it. What would that be?**

_____
_____
_____
_____
_____
_____

> 🍃 **What stops you from taking that action?**

_____
_____
_____
_____
_____
_____

> 🍃 **What needs to happen either within yourself or in your life situation for you to take the action to remedy this situation?**

_____
_____
_____
_____
_____
_____

For example, Erica worked part-time at a local restaurant to help meet the family's bills. She loved restaurant work but was frustrated in her role as a hostess/server. She wanted to be a "real" server in a good restaurant, with knowledge of foods and wines. It meant going to school, an expense that she felt would stretch the family's budget too thin. One night a fire destroyed the building next to her house. Her family had to run out of their home as they watched the flames come closer and closer to their own structure, eating the fence and lapping at the trees. Fortunately, the fire was stopped before it hit the house. The family did have to deal with smoke smells and some water damage, but they were grateful to have been otherwise untouched.

Erica decided that life was too unpredictable, that she couldn't wait until her children were all grown up and everyone was all settled before she pursued her dream. She talked to her husband and her older children. At first, none of them were particularly enthusiastic about making any changes. They liked life the way it was. Erica became relentless. Finally her family understood how important her dream was to Erica, and how ultimately it would benefit all of them, since she would have a much better income. They had a family meeting, and together they figured out how they could save a bit: her husband volunteered to take on some overtime, her oldest daughter volunteered to do some extra baby-sitting, and her son volunteered to deliver newspapers in the neighborhood so Erica could cut her hours at the restaurant. They borrowed some money from their savings. Erica went to school for a year and loved it. It was hard on her and on the family, but they also felt proud of themselves and their contribution.

If you feel that you need to make a change in your work situation, you might want to look at the following aspects of change:

> *Do you need to change your attitude in the situation that you are in? For example, not feeling that you must work through your lunch every day? Are you taking on more responsibility than necessary?*

Healing from Post-Traumatic Stress

🍃 What changes in the work situation would have to happen to help your present situation?

_____
_____
_____
_____

🍃 Can you ask for those changes that would make your present situation better? What would those be?

_____
_____
_____
_____

🍃 Do you need to find a way to get more recognition? A vacation? Take a sick leave? Request flextime? What do you need?

_____
_____
_____
_____

🍃 Do you need to change your place of work—find similar work in a different setting?

_____
_____
_____
_____

The Ripple Effect

_____

_____

_____

_____

Breathe! Trying to figure out what our work in the world is to be is an awesome endeavor. Take the time to rest, do some self-care, play! You might also consider connecting with a life coach to help you fine-tune your thoughts and your options.

Place of Residence

After a traumatic event you may find yourself questioning where you live. Thoughts and feelings may arise as to whether you should stay where you are or move to be in a more rural or urban setting.

Gabi lived in a small townhouse in a suburban setting near a large city. One night when she came home, she sensed that something was not right. She couldn't figure out what it was until she discovered that she had been burglarized. It was strange because there was no mess and most "normal" things had not been taken. Her jewelry was there, the twenty dollars that she had forgotten on the kitchen counter were there, the TV and stereo were in place. The only things missing were her laptop, her disks, and her papers, including her passport and other important documents. She was even more perplexed because she usually came home early on Thursday, but she had spontaneously decided to have dinner with a friend. She called the police. They couldn't tell her anything. None of her neighbors had heard anything, nor had any of them been burglarized.

Gabi, who was not yet an American citizen, was terrified. She thought that she was being stalked, but she didn't know who would do that. She was afraid of what would happen to her without her papers. How could she replace them? Could she get a new green card? She worried that it was a warning sign; would "they" (whoever they were) come after her? Fortunately, she had a good friend who took her in. Gabi could not be alone at all because she was so frightened. After a while she came to the realization that if whoever it was had wanted to harm her, he or she would have done so. But she still felt uncomfortable in her home, which until the incident had felt like a haven. She felt that she had to move.

Although Gabi realized that most likely it was not where she lived that was the problem, she couldn't stay there. The question was, where to go? Where could she feel safe? Finally she decided that being in a larger building with lots of people around would make her feel better. She sold her townhouse in the suburbs and moved into the city to an apartment on an upper floor in a large apartment building with doormen and security closed-circuit televisions. Gabi misses the air and the grass and the quiet, but feels that she is safe because no one can come in to what she refers to as "the fortress."

On the other hand, we have all seen the stories of the many people in New Orleans who, after Hurricane Katrina, said, "This is my home. I'm not going anywhere!" Again, there is no right or wrong. Your personal reactions depend on the type of trauma you have experienced and your personal situation vis-à-vis that event.

Write, draw, or make a collage of your thoughts and feelings regarding your place of residence. You can use photographs if you have some.

Healing from Post-Traumatic Stress

If you believe that you are living in the right place, take some time to look at the advantages of being where you are. It is always beneficial to recognize the good things in our lives.

✎ Why is where you are living the right place for you at this time?

- ☐ Convenience
  - ☐ to work
  - ☐ to schools
  - ☐ to relatives
  - ☐ to transportation
  - ☐ to recreation
- ☐ Spaciousness
- ☐ Friends
- ☐ Neighbors
- ☐ Price
- ☐ Surroundings
- ☐ Other:

_____

_____

_____

_____

If you feel that a geographical move would be beneficial, you might want to look at the following questions to help you determine why you feel that way and what type of setting would be more suitable for you at this time.

✎ What makes where you are living the wrong place for you at this time?

- ☐ The traumatic event
- ☐ The type of neighborhood
  - ☐ Did you feel it was the wrong place for you prior to the traumatic event?

The Ripple Effect

☐ Do you feel afraid there?
☐ Did the neighborhood change after the traumatic event?
☐ Too rural
☐ Too urban
☐ Everyone knows my business
☐ There's not enough support
☐ Too crowded
☐ It's not convenient
    ☐ to work
    ☐ to schools
    ☐ to shopping
    ☐ to family
    ☐ to friends
    ☐ to transportation
    ☐ to activities

Location

There are no "right" or "wrong" answers to any of the following questions. They are merely a guide to help you look at several of the considerations involved in making a geographical move. When thinking about a move, it is a good idea to let your imagination take over.

☞ *If you could have the perfect location, what would it be? An apartment in town? A small town? A large city? A rural setting?*

_____

_____

_____

☞ *What kind of neighborhood would you want? Sleepy and quiet? Busy and happening with lots of things to do? Ethnically diverse? Pretty homogeneous?*

_____

_____

Healing from Post-Traumatic Stress

> *What kind of place do you want to live in? A one-family house on some land? An apartment? A townhouse?*

_____

_____

_____

> *What sort of climate do you want to live in? A warm climate? A temperate climate? A cold climate?*

_____

_____

_____

> *Where do you want to live? The United States? A different country? Europe? Asia? Africa? Central or South America? The Middle East? Australia? Antarctica? The Caribbean? North America?*

_____

_____

_____

Thinking It Through

Once you've picked out the type of area that appeals to you, you might want to consider the following questions:

> *How would life be different there?*

_____

_____

_____

_____

The Ripple Effect

_____
_____
_____
_____

What would the advantages be?

_____
_____
_____
_____
_____

What would the disadvantages be?

_____
_____
_____
_____
_____

How would a move affect your work potential?

_____
_____
_____
_____
_____

Healing from Post-Traumatic Stress

☞ **How would a move affect your personal life and relationships with family and friends?**

_____
_____
_____
_____
_____
_____
_____

☞ **Any other considerations?**

_____
_____
_____
_____
_____
_____

As you review your thoughts and feelings about these questions, remember to take your time, consider your options, research other communities and different lifestyles, and visit a variety of places that appeal to you. If you are unsure how to make the change, you can contact a relocation specialist, ask your friends and acquaintances who live in different places, or contact a real estate broker in areas that might be of interest.

If you possibly can, spend some time in your ideal setting. Maybe you can rent a place for a while. Talk to the people who live there. Do you feel comfortable with them? Does that place have the kind of activities that are important to you? Will you be able to find work? Schools? Sometimes our fantasies and the realities of the situation are not the same.

A personal story: Many years ago, I decided that I wanted to experiment with living in the country. I love the outdoors and thought it would be wonderful to live there. We found a cute little house nestled in the woods, near a creek. My dream come true! It was close enough to the city that I could come back a couple of days a week to see clients. Perfect!

Fortunately, we had not relinquished our city abode (more luck than not, as we had been unable to sell it). I loved the outdoors, true. But I hated that I had to get into the car to do grocery shopping, that I couldn't go to the corner deli to pick up the quart of milk I had forgotten when doing the rest of the shopping. I missed public transportation. I couldn't stand that I had to drive a half hour or more to see my friends instead of walking a few blocks. So we moved back into the city.

My friend Halima, on the other hand, moved out to the country and loved it. She didn't mind the commute; she didn't mind all the things that I had hated. She didn't mind that she didn't have the type of lifestyle that she had had in the city. She didn't miss her activities, she didn't feel lonely. She's still there.

Make time for a pause. Thinking about relocation can feel overwhelming; there are so many things to consider. Remember, you don't have to do it all at once. You now have the rough sketch of what you'd like to see in the future. This is a good beginning. Also, looking at places to live may have brought up many memories: some good, some not so good. Honor whatever you are feeling, and make sure to take some time for self-care.

Interests, Hobbies, and Activities

These pages invite you to reflect on your interests, hobbies, and activities. Have you noticed any changes in your interests and activities since the trauma? Some of the ways you spent your time may now seem unimportant to you (like going to the mall), while others may seem more precious (like spending the morning with your family doing puzzles). You may also be drawn to new experiences and new activities. Possibly some interest, hobby, or activity that you used to enjoy and gave up on is calling you back.

Or maybe you've grown interested in pursuing an activity that you always wanted to try but never found the time or courage for.

Nala, a colleague of mine, got mugged coming home late from work. She was really shaken up. She works in an impoverished neighborhood and does amazing work with troubled kids, many of them gang members. Even though it was a "bad" neighborhood, she felt that she was known in the community and that no one would attack her. But there it was—she was being mugged at knifepoint. Fortunately, she was not hurt. The muggers took her watch and her wallet and left her unharmed but shaken.

She made her way home and knew enough about trauma not to go it alone. She called a couple of friends, and we went to her house and did what friends do: we made tea, called the police to report the incident, listened to her tell the story over and over, fed her, told her it would be okay (although she didn't believe us!), and stayed until morning when she had stopped crying and shaking.

Being a clinician, Nala went immediately for crisis counseling, which then evolved into her reassessing her priorities. She realized that she could have died that night and that as much as she wanted to be of help to the people she worked with, she had neglected herself and her own family and friends. Nala remembered all the things that she used to do before she took this job: concerts and dances and museum exhibits and dinners with those she loved. She set a new schedule for herself that she would not work late more than two evenings a week and that she would not bring work home unless it was an emergency.

To make sure that she stuck to her decision, she signed up for a music appreciation class. She also wanted to feel less vulnerable out there in the streets and signed up for martial arts classes twice a week.

✍ *Write, draw, and/or make a collage of your interests, hobbies, and activities prior to your trauma.*

Healing from Post-Traumatic Stress

Which of those pursuits are you still engaged in?

_____

_____

_____

_____

_____

Which of those pursuits have you given up?

_____

_____

_____

_____

_____

Why?

_____

_____

_____

_____

_____

You may have given up many of your activities because they have lost their appeal and you were looking to realign your priorities and seek out new projects. However, make sure that you have ceased these pursuits to make room for something else (like spending more time at home with your family), and not because you are feeling lethargic, uninterested, and unmotivated. If you find that you have given up many of your activities and lost interest in activities that you once found enjoyable, without wanting to explore new ones, it could be a sign of post-traumatic stress disorder, and it would be a good idea to seek help.

As already mentioned several times, trauma is often a "wake-up call." Going through a traumatic event often makes us examine our lives and propels us to healthier choices. Perhaps you have a newfound desire to give up unhealthy activities like staying out at the bar till all hours of the morning, driving at one hundred miles an hour, gambling, or getting into debt.

List the interests, hobbies, and activities that you want to give up.

_____
_____
_____
_____
_____
_____

What propels you to do so?

_____
_____
_____
_____
_____
_____

If you are trying to give up a negative or harmful activity and are having trouble, take a few minutes to consider what makes it difficult.

_____
_____

_____

_____

_____

_____

_____

> *Use the space below to jot down what might help you give up those activities. If those activities involve drugs or alcohol, there are many free programs such as AA and NA that can help.*

_____

_____

_____

_____

_____

_____

Like Nala, many trauma survivors find that they want to make changes in their life. One of the facets of these changes is how to occupy one's time. What interests call to you? What feels nurturing? Satisfying? Exciting? Productive? Connecting?

The following exercise asks you to imagine what kind of activities you might like to explore. Maybe they are interests that you've always had, like Nala's interest in music, or maybe they are new endeavors, like Nala's martial arts classes.

> *List interests, hobbies, and activities that you would like to explore.*

_____

_____

_____

_____

_____

The Ripple Effect

What prevents you from doing so? Many of us have an idea of something we want to do, whether it is to take a class, stay home and read the papers, make a quilt, learn how to do Sudoku or crossword puzzles, knit a scarf, spend time in the shed puttering with things to fix, repaint the living room, or bake a cake, yet we don't do it. This exercise is a bit of a push to help you look at your resistance to doing what you really want to do.

_____

_____

_____

_____

_____

_____

_____

_____

What needs to happen for you to pursue these interests? Do you need to have a conversation about time with your partner, or maybe get him or her to come with you? Do you need to do a little bit of research to find out where the classes are? Do you need a little push from a friend who will show you the way? This exercise will help you clarify what needs to happen for you to pursue a desired interest and maybe also reveal a little bit of what your resistance to taking the plunge might be.

_____

_____

_____

_____

_____

_____

_____

_____

How can you overcome these obstacles? It might be helpful to talk to some-one who can help you move through your resistance and encourage you to go ahead. This is also a time when having a couple of sessions with a coun-selor or life coach could be helpful.

A Note of Caution

Occasionally after a traumatic experience people are drawn to high-risk activities. If you find yourself wanting to do high-adventure activities that were not previously part of your lifestyle, like solo rock climbing, motorcycle racing, skydiving, or going on "Survivor," please take some time to consider whether this is the right activity for you or whether this desire stems from an unhealthy, "what the heck, it doesn't matter anyway" attitude or a challenge to life. If you still feel you want to try one of these activities, be cautious and make sure that you do it in a safe, appropriate fashion.

You may have found new ways of occupying your time that feel more nurturing and rewarding than the ones you had before, and you may be feel-ing good about that. On the other hand, the exercises in this chapter may have brought up some difficult thoughts and feelings. You may have had to give up hobbies and interests for reasons other than choice. Like Kevin in the previous chapter, physical injuries may prevent you from doing what you used to do, and there may still be grief or resentment around that. If that is the case, you might want to revisit Chapter 8 and find a professional who can help you move through your grief so that, like Kevin, you can go on with satisfying pursuits.

Congratulations! With this series of exercises, you have completed a long, intense, and complicated journey into your life. At this moment, take a breather, do some self-care activity, and remember that whatever came up for you during any of the exercises is a trailhead to the new paths that await you. There is no rush, no deadlines. Good luck on your journey.

◢

While changes in relationships, work, and activities are normal after a trauma, there are times when these changes are indicative of a larger problem. There are a few red flags that I would like to highlight for you:

- You find that many of your relationships are difficult but were not before.
- You have no interest in your work, but you did before.
- You want to move, but can't figure out why or where.
- You find that you have given up most of the activities, hobbies, and interests that you used to have and have no desire to replace them with anything else.
- You find yourself engaging in high-risk activities or behaviors, especially those involving drugs, alcohol, promiscuity, or any other hurtful behaviors.

If you are facing any of these symptoms and behaviors intensely, or have been experiencing them over a period of a couple of months or more, it might be helpful for you to seek counseling from a therapist or a religious adviser. If you don't know anyone, refer to the section "Finding Help" in the Introduction to this book.

11

People Close to You: Family and Friends

"Shared joy is a double joy. Shared sorrow is half a sorrow."
—Swedish adage

Most of us are not isolated beings, and in most instances, what happens to us affects those around us. So even though you are the one to whom the trauma happened, the ripples are felt by those around you, and most noticeably by those closest to you. These individuals are commonly known as secondary victims. Usually, though not always, the closer the connection between you and that other person, the greater the impact your trauma has on him or her.

In some instances, your close ones went through the same trauma at the same time as you did. As a result, you may have a new, positive feeling of connectedness with them. Although this is not necessarily so, a profound sense of camaraderie and belonging often develops when people go through rough times together. The same is true for good times! This bonding may last only a short time, although for some people it can last a lifetime.

Other individuals who weren't there with you may be struggling with difficult feelings related to what happened to you, a form of survivor's guilt. They may also feel excluded from the bond that has formed between those of you who were there: this is called the in/out syndrome.

Some individuals close to you may have a knack of knowing how to comfort and support you. Those people intuitively know what kind of emotional and practical help you need and what forms it needs to take. For example, after Irina's husband left her, she felt that she had lost everything. Besides feeling thrown aside and rejected, she lost her status and her financial security. In addition, because her husband was the head of their spiritual community, she felt excluded from her place of solace. Irina is not from this country originally, so she didn't even have a family to fall back on (not, as she mentioned, that they wouldn't have blamed her for her failure to keep her husband). Fortunately, she had two good friends who took her under their wings. They intuitively knew how to be of help. They made sure that she had a place to go for holidays, and they included her in their activities, invited her for dinner at least once a week, and asked her to help with shopping, wallpapering, quilting, or whatever so she would not feel embarrassed to take their help and so she would not be alone on weekends.

Other individuals close to you may be involved in their own healing, and thus may not be available to you. Or they simply may not have what it takes to be sympathetic or supportive. On the contrary, they may behave in ways that are upsetting to you. They may turn out not to be the people you expected them to be. This can be disappointing, upsetting, frustrating, and even scary: you may have counted on a person to be there for you, and he or she is not! For example, some of Irina's old friends started avoiding her. One of them, Wila, literally told Irina that she could no longer be friends with her now that she was divorced. (Irina later found out that one of those friends' marriage was in trouble, and she found it too scary to hear about Irina's distress and struggles.)

As happened with Wila, your trauma may be a trigger for something in a friend or relative. Although your friend or relative did not go through the same ordeal that you did, what happened to you may have triggered something for this person, usually an unhealed trauma of her or his own. Ironically, this person may be feeling about you the same way you are feeling about her or him, wondering why you are not being more supportive or comforting.

This chapter invites you to take a look at how the people in your life have been impacted by your trauma and how this might be informing the way that they are responding to you. The following is a list of reactions that victims of trauma often experience from people close to them. Feel free to check those that apply, skip those that don't, and add any not included. Some reactions may apply to some friends and relatives and different ones to others; you might want to ascribe the reaction to the appropriate person.

Reaction	From Whom?
Loving	_____
Overbearing	_____
Caring	_____
Overprotective	_____
Distancing	_____
Aloof	_____
More connected	_____
Mean	_____
Kind	_____
Helpful	_____
Angry	_____
Blaming	_____
Understanding	_____
Impatient ("get over it already")	_____
Patient	_____
Demanding	_____
Comforting	_____
Fearful	_____
Shy	_____
Full of advice	_____
Don't know what to say	_____
Overemotional	_____
Other:	_____

_____   _____

_____   _____

_____   _____

_____   _____

Some people may feel guilty or even somehow responsible for what happened to you. This sometimes prevents them from being supportive after your trauma. They feel guilty for having done or not done something that they believe might have prevented the trauma. Therefore, when they see you having a hard time, it becomes a reminder of their ineptitude and becomes too much for them to bear. The only way they know to deal with it may be by avoiding you or blaming you.

Some people may be angry with you for having "put yourself" in a situation they disapprove of, and therefore will withhold support—the "I told you so" crowd. Those people hold to the belief "if you made your bed, you can lie in it," even if the trauma was random. For example, Maria was hit by a car and injured badly on her way home from the library one evening. Her father was furious with her because he had told her that she couldn't go out with boys and stay out at night. He absolutely refused to believe that she had been at the library, even when friends vouched for her.

Sometimes remembering personal trauma enhances people's capacity to be present, understanding, and compassionate toward others—hence, the success of self-help groups. Conversely, some people may be impeded by their own trauma from handling any issue on your part that feels threatening to their own stability or that comes too close to what they are going through themselves.

Finally, there are people who do not have the capacity for compassion and service. They may be so self-involved that they can't see that anyone else exists. If you are faced with people like that, there is nothing you can do but recognize that those people are who they are and it is useless to try to connect with them or ask anything of them. Tonia and her husband had had a very hard time conceiving. She was getting older and was concerned about her biological clock. Finally, she became pregnant. She and her husband were ecstatic. Then she miscarried. They were crushed. They felt they had lost their last chance to have a child. When Tonia told her mother-in-law, the latter said, "Oh, you'll get over it. I had a miscarriage before I had my four children," totally insensitive to Tonia's feelings and to the dissimilarity of their circumstances.

Write, make a list, draw, and/or make a collage of how your trauma has affected the people close to you.

Does the information you gathered in the preceding exercise help you understand certain people's attitudes and behaviors toward you? If so, what have you learned?

Name of Person   **What You Learned**

_____   _____
_____   _____
_____   _____
_____   _____
_____   _____
_____   _____

If not, what is still puzzling to you?

Name of Person   **What Is Confusing or Puzzling**

_____   _____
_____   _____
_____   _____
_____   _____
_____   _____
_____   _____

Additionally, some people hold a rigid code of beliefs and behaviors that may prevent their being available to you. It may not be a lack of caring or concern, but a strongly held view of how matters should be handled. My paternal grandmother, known in the family as the "Grande Dame" (great lady), had lost her husband when she was very young and lived through two wars, and she held the belief that one should never show weakness, which meant no crying, no complaining about pain, nothing that would spoil a composed image. She never showed compassion to anyone, except maybe my father. As a little girl I thought she was mean and hated me. Later, I learned that she adored me and wanted to make sure that I would acquire the right ways of handling life.

Healing from Post-Traumatic Stress

Check off those personal beliefs that might be held by your family, friends, or acquaintances that would inhibit them from being supportive to you.

Belief   **Family, Friend, or Acquaintance**

Keep a stiff upper lip   _____

Don't dwell on it   _____

Be strong   _____

Get over it   _____

Put it in a drawer and forget it   _____

No point in rehashing   _____

Go on with your life   _____

Other:

_____   _____

_____   _____

_____   _____

_____   _____

_____   _____

_____   _____

This section is provided for you to examine the reactions of those close to you and those with whom you interact routinely. I hope that looking at each relationship will help you to understand why one person can be helpful and comforting to you, while another cannot. As you examine each relationship, please remember that the person you are focusing on may be going through her or his own predicament. This understanding might help you feel better about the situation and improve your relationship to that person.

For example, Reuben was very upset. A very bright, ambitious young man, he didn't like things not to go his way. He had gotten into a bad car accident that had totaled his car. Fortunately, he only had a bruised forehead, some burns on his arms from the air bag, and a hairline fracture to one of his ribs. Reuben was very angry with his friend Daniel, who was not answering his calls promptly, not volunteering to take him places, and altogether not being available for support.

I suggested to Reuben that maybe Daniel was having some issues of his own to deal with. Reuben would not hear of it and decided to stop talking to Daniel. A few days later he heard from Daniel. Daniel's mother had suddenly died of a stroke, and he had been told that there was a good chance he would lose his job, as his company was being restructured. Reuben was embarrassed that he had judged his friend so badly, and although there was still a small part of him that was still angry at not having gotten his needs met, he was able to put that aside and be there for his friend in his time of loss.

The following chart will help you clarify what your expectations were from different people in your life and what you did or did not receive from them. If they have not met your expectations, what might be the cause of it—what might be going on with each person that prevents her or him from helping meet your needs?

Person	Your Expectations	What You Did or Did Not Receive	What Might Be the Cause?
Partners	_____	_____	_____
Parents	_____	_____	_____
Children	_____	_____	_____
Friends	_____	_____	_____
Neighbors	_____	_____	_____
Coworkers	_____	_____	_____
Other:			
_____	_____	_____	_____
_____	_____	_____	_____
_____	_____	_____	_____
_____	_____	_____	_____
_____	_____	_____	_____
_____	_____	_____	_____

Are there any surprises to what you found out? Did you discover, as with Reuben and Daniel, that someone whom you thought was just not caring of you was so overwhelmed by her or his own problems that there was not enough emotional or physical energy to give to anyone else?

_____
_____
_____
_____
_____

It might be helpful to both of you if you could check in with the people you listed to see what is going on with them. You might then be able to support and comfort each other.

Think about whom you would like to talk to and what you would say to them:

Who	**What Would You Like to Say?**
_____	_____
_____	_____
_____	_____
_____	_____
_____	_____

I hope that by looking at these exercises, you have clarified what you expect from your family, friends, and coworkers and whom you can count on for what.

If you are getting what you need, fabulous! If not, there are several options:

- Ask for what you need—you might be quite surprised by the positive response.
- Realize that the particular person you hoped would be helpful cannot fulfill your need, and reach out to someone else.
- *Do not* decide that there is something wrong with you, or with the other person, because you are not getting what you need.

Asking for help and accepting support might be difficult for you. However, particularly after a traumatic event, it is a good idea to find a way to get support. The following chapter will help you to recognize the importance of asking for help and how to go about doing so, because there is no need to go through post-traumatic stress alone.

It is unlikely, however, that all your needs will be met by one person, or even several. So your balancing act will be to reach out to have your needs met and recognize that no one can totally take care of you or do the work of healing for you.

As we come to the end of this chapter, take some time to settle into the information that you have just gleaned, relax a bit, and transition back to your everyday life.

12

You Don't Have to Do It Alone

"If I am not for myself, who will be for me?
If I am not for others, what am I?
And if not now, when?"

—Rabbi Hillel

Many people find solace in the company of others. Conversely, many people prefer solitude. They would rather work things out on their own, and they find others an intrusion and a bother. Honor your own predilection. If you need to withdraw from people and gather into yourself to heal, do that. If you prefer to reach out to people, do that. Also remember that you can do both, depending on the situation.

You may have come from a background, culture, or upbringing that values communality, where people are expected to take care of each other. In that case, you may have a solid cooperative network; giving and receiving support may be a usual aspect of your everyday life. This chapter can serve as a guide to organize what you would like help with and who might be the best person or persons to ask.

At the other end of the spectrum, you may have come from a belief system, culture, or upbringing that emphasizes self-reliance. In that case, asking for help can be quite a challenge. You may feel embarrassed and self-conscious, or you may tell yourself that you should be able to do it on your own.

Finally, for whatever reason, you may not have a support network that you can call upon for help—maybe you are new in town, maybe you are shy, maybe you tend to prefer being alone and have not developed a network, maybe you don't trust that the people you know would be willing to help, or any of many other reasons. If that is the case, there are many groups and agencies that can provide you with some of the backing that you might need. I encourage you to take steps to find the help you need. Going through the aftermath of a trauma alone is extremely difficult. Please refer to the Introduction of this book for information on how to find help.

It Takes Strength and Courage to Ask for Help

I believe that asking for help is a sign of strength because it honors our humanness. I also believe that asking for what you need is actually a gift to the person you ask. Most people would like to be available to someone who is going through a difficult time but have no idea what to do or even what to say. Your willingness to ask for help provides you with what you need and also helps others feel they have made a valuable contribution.

After Anna's son was run over by a car, her friends all wanted to say or do something that would help. They just had no idea what. They couldn't just keep asking, "How are you doing?" and "Do you need anything?" Anna was in "super-function mode." "I'm fine," she kept saying, "I'm handling it." But her friends could tell she wasn't coping all that well. Finally, they took it upon themselves to take action. They got together and went to see Anna and presented her with their plan. One person was going to do her shopping, another was going to clean her house, another was going to make needed phone calls, another offered to help write thank-you notes to the people who had come to the funeral, and they all offered to drop in periodically during the week while her husband and children were out of the house.

At first Anna kept saying, "I'm fine. Ed and I are handling this." But as her friends continued to gently insist, she broke down and finally allowed herself to be comforted and taken care of. Not only was it a wonderful healing for Anna, who had never received any support from her family, but it also helped her friends feel good about themselves and bonded these women into a loving, tight-knit group that has now weathered many tragedies together, giving to and receiving from each other.

After a traumatic event there may be many things you need help with. It can be anything from buying groceries, getting to work, dealing with government or medical agencies, completing paperwork, making phone calls, or cleaning your house to having a sympathetic ear. Some years ago a friend went through some serious surgery and several follow-up surgeries. She organized several of her friends to help. Some of us took turns taking her to the hospital, some of us cooked, others went clothes shopping, someone took charge of the paperwork, and several people had a housecleaning party. Because each person did a little bit, no one felt overwhelmed and our friend felt really well taken care of. And we were delighted to be able to help her in the ways that she needed, rather than trying to guess what to do.

The following pages invite you to recognize and organize what you need help with and whom you can call upon according to each person's skills and availability. For example, Sabrina might be great to get your paperwork organized, but doesn't have the patience to listen to what is on your mind. Frank, on the other hand, can listen to you for as long as you need to talk, but has no organizational skills. You can call Tasha for a ride anywhere, at any time, but don't ask her to go into a store or make a phone call, and you can count on Miriam to get everyone organized. If each person on your list does a little bit, then no one will be overburdened.

It sometimes happens that the people you ask for help can't give it. That can feel hurtful and disappointing. There are a variety of reasons why that might happen. Remember, though, that most of the time when people refuse to help, it is not because of you but because of something going on in their own life that you may not know about (like Reuben and his friend Daniel), or it might be an aspect of their personality.

The next exercise invites you to take a look at how you feel about asking for help, and what those beliefs are based on. The following ones encourage you to look at your needs in the different areas of your life and to pair those needs with those individuals who might be best suited for each task. As with all the other exercises in the book, take your time and be gentle with yourself.

☞ *If it is easy for you to ask for help, draw, write, and/or make a collage to express what those beliefs are based on.*

🍃 **If it is difficult for you to ask for help, write, draw, and/or make a collage of what makes it so for you.**

Healing from Post-Traumatic Stress

> *Write a few sentences about where your beliefs related to asking for help came from. For instance, "My grandmother always told me not to involve other people in my business."*

_____
_____
_____
_____
_____
_____
_____

> *Are the reasons upon which those beliefs are based still true? If so, how? Or are those reasons antiquated and in need of renovation?*

_____
_____
_____
_____
_____
_____
_____

There may be a multitude of reasons why asking for help is not your style. Paolo came from a large, volatile family. More often than not, asking for help would get him into trouble or berated, or both. So he learned very young to take care of himself and not make waves. Once when playing with friends he got hit on the head with a board and started bleeding profusely. Used to taking care of things, he put ice on it, stopped the bleeding, and that was it for him. Later on he told his sister about it. She in turn told his father, who spanked him for having gotten into trouble. His mother then went into hysterics about how he might have died, saying they should sue the other boys.

This anchored Paolo's belief that letting people know what was going on with him or asking for help was more complicated and ultimately more painful than handling things on his own.

Following is a list of possibilities of why you might not feel comfortable asking for help. Check off those that apply to you, and add any others that fit your situation.

- ☐ We don't wash our dirty laundry in public.
- ☐ What goes on with you is not anybody else's business.
- ☐ I don't want people to feel sorry for me.
- ☐ I don't need help. I can do it on my own.
- ☐ If I ask for help, I'll just get disappointed again.
- ☐ You can't trust people.
- ☐ People will think less of me.
- ☐ I don't want my privacy invaded.
- ☐ I can do it myself.
- ☐ I don't know whom to ask.
- ☐ It's just easier to deal with it myself.
- ☐ I don't want to deal with other people's reactions.
- ☐ I'll have to pay for it later.
- ☐ Others:

_____

_____

_____

_____

All of the reasons you checked are valid and make sense to you. However, it is my experience that ultimately it is beneficial not to go it alone. I invite you to look at the following exercises to see if any of the suggestions given make sense to you.

Asking for Help

The following exercise is aimed at creating a template from which you can determine who is the best person to ask for what.

Make a list of people in your support network. Include relatives, friends, and other people such as coworkers, clergy, doctors, therapists, teachers, and neighbors—anyone who might be able to play a part in your recovery. Next to each name write that person's strong point. It's okay if you don't have someone for each line, and it is equally fine if you have more.

Your Support Network

If you feel a bit uncomfortable here and think that you don't have a support network, I invite you to stretch your imagination a bit. Maybe your neighbor with the dog who gets the paper every morning wouldn't mind picking up something for you on his way. Or maybe that coworker who lives a few blocks away would be willing to pick you up on her way from work.

Name   **Skills or Abilities**

_____   _____
_____   _____
_____   _____
_____   _____
_____   _____
_____   _____
_____   _____
_____   _____
_____   _____
_____   _____
_____   _____
_____   _____
_____   _____

Make a specific list of the practical things you want help with. Write everything down, even the little things. One of the aftereffects of having gone through a traumatic experience is that everything can feel overwhelming, even things that you were perfectly capable of handling on your own prior to the event. I remember a very difficult time in my own life when I looked into the refrigerator and found I was out of milk. It was overwhelming. I couldn't bear the thought of having to go out to the corner to get a bottle. It's normal and appropriate to have such feelings. Let yourself get help, and you will return to your level of self-sufficiency faster. Next to each thing that needs doing, write down the person or people who could do it. Feel free to add more lines if you need them.

Practical Action or Activity　　　　**Who Can Help?**

　　　　　　Healing from Post-Traumatic Stress

Now make a list of your emotional needs. These are as important as your practical needs. For example, having someone spend time with you, go out to dinner or a movie, go for a walk, come over and talk, and so on. It doesn't have to be big.

Emotional Need	Who Can Provide It?

Kudos! You have taken another step on your path to recovery. Regardless of what these exercises revealed to you, it was a gift: either you discovered that certain old beliefs no longer make sense in your life, and that's good news; or you might have ascertained that the way you do your life works for you, and that's good news as well.

As with so many of the exercises in this book, the ones you just completed might have felt comforting, or they might have brought up painful feelings. You might be surprised by the richness of your support network, or you might be feeling sad that there aren't many people close to you to reach out to at this time. Either way, this knowledge gives you options to feel grateful for what you have and find ways to create what you don't.

If you feel that you don't have a good support network, but you don't quite know how to begin to create one, you can look for an existing one. Many organizations, such as community centers, Ys, Neighborhood Houses, or the Self-Help Clearinghouse, have information on all types of support groups and people who are willing to help.

No matter how this chapter impacted you, take some time to reorient yourself, to do something loving and caring before you go on to the tasks of the day.

13

Medical and Psychological Attention

Regardless of how long it has been since your trauma, you should neglect neither your physical nor your mental well-being. You may be just fine, and there may be no need for you to seek either physical or emotional treatment. However, as in the case of Anna in the last chapter, we may think that we are fine when we are not quite. I recommend that you revisit Chapter 3 to make sure that you are not dealing with PTS symptoms that you would rather not know are there. Also, if you are noticing that people close to you keep asking if you are okay, there may be a grain of salt in what they are seeing or feeling in you. If you are truly feeling well physically and emotionally, only do the exercises that relate to the treatment you received, or skip this chapter altogether.

The following pages are intended to help you do the following:

- Reflect on any medical and psychological attention that you have received after your trauma (Although health practitioners intend the best, the treatment received, especially at hospitals and clinics, can often be quite upsetting and traumatizing in and of itself.)
- Decide if it would be a good idea to seek professional services for either your physical body or your emotional well-being
- Find referrals

Your Physical Well-Being

Depending on the type of trauma that you went through, you may have been immediately taken to a hospital or clinic for treatment or observation. On the other hand, you may not have shown any symptoms and may not have been seen. Let's say you were in a car accident, and you didn't feel hurt at the time, or not that badly. You might have chosen not to seek medical attention.

Whatever the case, I encourage you to pay attention to your body. Have there been changes since your trauma? Headaches? Digestive problems? Aches and pains? Shortness of breath? Any other symptoms that were not present before the trauma? If you have anything unusual going on with your body, do check with a health provider.

If you have received medical treatment, the next section is for you. If you have not received medical treatment, skip the next section and start with the following section, "If You Have Not Received Medical Care."

If You Have Received or Are Receiving Medical Care

You may have been taken to a hospital, clinic, or doctor immediately after the trauma or shortly thereafter, or you may have chosen to seek medical attention on your own at a later time.

Regardless of the circumstances, the following questions are meant as an overview of your experience, whether it was positive or negative.

The facility was/is: _____

_____

The staff was/is: _____

_____

The nurses were/are:_____

_____

I'm glad that the paramedics, staff, nurses, doctors, etc., were/are:

_____

_____

I wish that the paramedics, staff, nurses, doctors were: _____

_____

_____

The doctors were/are: _____

_____

Do you feel comfortable with your doctor? If so, what makes you feel that way? _____

_____

_____

If not, what makes you feel that way? _____

_____

_____

Do you feel that your doctor is competent? _____

_____

If not, what keeps you going back to that practitioner? _____

_____

_____

If you are still in need of medical care and do not like the physician who has been caring for you, it is perfectly acceptable to find someone you like better. Regardless of your situation, there are many, many providers who can be of help, and you do not need to stay with one you do not like. Furthermore, if you have any concerns or questions about your treatment, it is quite appropriate to get a second or even a third opinion.

Healing from Post-Traumatic Stress

If You Have Not Received Medical Care

Some individuals are quick to seek medical care, others are more reluctant. The reasons can range from family and cultural patterns to financial situation or personal beliefs about medical care.

Why have you not sought medical attention? _____
_____
_____

Note any physical symptoms, regardless of how minor, that you have had since your trauma. These could include digestive problems, trouble sleeping, headaches, muscle aches, or any other physical effects you are experiencing (you might want to refer back to the lists in Chapter 3 for more possible symptoms). _____
_____
_____

If you are having physical symptoms, what is preventing you from getting medical attention? _____
_____
_____

What would need to happen for you to seek attention for your symptoms? For example, do you need medical insurance, a referral to a doctor, or something else? _____
_____
_____

How can you make that happen? _____
_____
_____

Is there someone who could be instrumental in helping you get medical attention? (A good place to start would be your support network from Chapter 12.)

Name: _____

Name: _____

Name: _____

Your Emotional Well-Being

As I have mentioned many times throughout the book, going through a trauma can affect you emotionally—sometimes immediately after the trauma, sometimes later on. Pay attention to your moods and how you are feeling overall. If you find that your moods and feelings are impacting negatively on your life, do check with a mental health provider. It is important for your overall healing that you be emotionally well.

If you have received psychological treatment, the next section is for you. If you have not received psychological treatment, skip the next section and start with the following section, "If You Have Not Received Psychological Care."

If You Have Received or Are Receiving Psychological Treatment

What prompted you to do so? _____
_____
_____

How was/is the assistance that you received/are receiving? _____
_____

Do you feel the person you are seeing understands you? _____
_____

Do you feel comfortable with that person? If so, what about that person makes you feel safe and comfortable? _____

Healing from Post-Traumatic Stress

If not, what makes you feel uncomfortable? _____

_____

_____

If you are not at ease with that person, what keeps you there? _____

_____

_____

Do you feel that person is knowledgeable about trauma? _____

_____

What do you wish that person would do? _____

_____

_____

What do you wish that person would not do? _____

_____

_____

It is absolutely acceptable to ask the person that you are seeing for what you need. It is also a good idea to let that person know what you wish she or he would or would not do. Most mental health providers are sensitive, but they are not mind readers. It is not a sign of disrespect for you to ask for what you need. On the contrary, it helps your practitioner be more attuned to you and to understand you better.

When working with a mental health provider, it is really important to be with the right person for you, as a large part of psychological healing comes out of the relationship with your provider. You should feel safe, accepted, respected, and cared about. I always suggest to people that they should "shop" until they find the right match. Moreover, it is essential to remember that emotional healing is a process that is subtle, at times even unnoticeable. Unlike a physical wound that we can watch heal, emotional healing is less visible. Healing from trauma usually takes at least four seasons, or a full year, so give yourself the gift of patience.

Vinny had just come back from serving in the military in Iraq. He had left home enthused at the idea of serving his country and bringing democracy and peace to the Middle East. When he returned two years later, he was angry and frightened. He had seen things that he couldn't talk about and felt things that he never imagined possible. He had nightmares and flashbacks, and he didn't know how to relate to his young wife and felt lost as a civilian. He felt like everything in life was a lie. He didn't know what he wanted to do in his life. He had studied to be an EMT, but now didn't know if he could keep working with people who were dying. He also felt guilty that he had not been hurt physically, as several of his buddies had been wounded and a few had died.

Vinny had never thought he would be in therapy. But here he was. He worked hard at putting the pieces of his life back together, but he often felt frustrated that he wasn't back to his old self. He felt that he took two steps forward, one step back. He was starting to believe that life would never be okay again. In working with him I kept repeating that healing takes time, but he was getting weary of hearing that.

Then, about nine months after we had started our work together, he came into the office and said, "A funny thing happened last week. I didn't have a nightmare. I slept through the night except for once." From that day on, Vinny's healing accelerated. He found a way to put his experience into a larger perspective of his life. He reconnected with his love of helping people and went back to work at the hospital. He and his wife decided they needed to restart their marriage and went on a second honeymoon.

It hasn't been all roses for Vinny, but slowly he's re-created a life that works for him and his family. He still has some nightmares and flashbacks when something triggers his memory of Iraq, but he knows how to work with them so they don't take over. He can't watch the news on TV, but as he says, "There's worse things in life than not watching the news—at least I can watch the sports!"

If you need psychological care and you do not like the practitioner who has been caring for you, it is perfectly acceptable to find someone you like better. Regardless of your situation, there are many providers who can be of help, and you do not need to stay with one you do not like.

Write, draw, and/or make a collage of your thoughts and feelings about the emotional attention that you have received/are receiving.

If You Have Not Received Psychological Care

Just as some people can easily reach out to a medical doctor and others not, some people can easily reach out to a mental health practitioner or counselor and others find it difficult. The same basic reasons apply, ranging from belief system to finances and cultural mores. However, it is important that you not neglect your mental well-being. It is as important to be emotionally healthy as it is to be physically well.

Some individuals feel that it is shameful to seek psychological help or that only those with severe problems see a mental health practitioner or counselor. This is far from the truth. People all over the world rely on mental health professionals for all types of problems, including how to deal with their children, how to manage their relationship with their spouse, how to resolve matters with neighbors and relatives, how to deal with birth and illness and death, and how to cope with the difficulties of life in general. Mental health practitioners have existed for millennia under various names. In tribal societies they were called medicine women or shamans; later on, the members of the clergy ministered advice (they still do, and are a good resource); and medical doctors used to know the lives of their patients, listen to their life problems, and help them resolve them. As medicine became more specialized, a group of professionals became specialized in the art of helping people with emotional problems. Those are the psychotherapists and counselors of today.

The following exercises are a road map to help you determine if it would be wise for you to seek mental health support.

Note any emotions or mood swings that you are having since your trauma. If you are uncertain, look at the list of symptoms in Chapter 3.

> ☞ **If you are having some emotional issues that affect your everyday life, what would need to happen for you to seek emotional support?**

_____
_____
_____
_____
_____
_____

> ☞ **How could you make that happen?**

_____
_____
_____
_____
_____
_____

Is there someone who could be of help in finding a mental health practitioner for you? (A good place to start would be your support network from Chapter 12.)

Name: _____

Name: _____

Referrals

There are many ways to find the appropriate practitioner, whether it is for physical care or for psychological treatment. If the very thought of having to look for a practitioner feels overwhelming, or if you are having a hard time finding the right fit for you, ask someone from your list in the section "Your

Support Network" in Chapter 12 to help you out, or refer to the Introduction of this book for advice on how to get help.

If you have a primary physician that you like, she or he is a good person to ask for a referral. The old "birds of a feather" adage applies here, as like-minded people will usually know one another and refer to each other. The same holds true if you like and trust your spiritual leader. These people often have developed a network of practitioners to whom they will refer you. You can ask a friend, a relative, or a coworker for a recommendation as well. Just make sure that whomever you connect with is the right person for you. It might feel overwhelming to go shopping for help, but in the end it will make your life so much easier to have the right fit.

If for some reason none of the sources I have mentioned appeals to you, you can contact agencies that might be of help. They are bound by rules of confidentiality, so your request will be kept absolutely private. The following broad categories of agencies should be able to supply you with suitable referrals:

- Hospitals
- Religion-based organizations such as Catholic Charities (catholic charitiesinfo.org) and Jewish Community Service. YM/YWCAs and YM/YWHAs also sometimes have referral services.
- The National Mental Health Consumers' Self-Help Clearinghouse (mhselfhelp.org or 800-553-4539)
- Crime victims' boards and victim assistance services: even if you are not a crime victim, they sometimes have referral lists or can point you to an agency that might help.
- The Red Cross
- Community centers

If the listed resources do not help, you can try the Yellow Pages. It is not possible from that kind of a listing to determine if a practitioner is qualified, so if you do utilize the Yellow Pages, be sure to check the practitioner's credentials. See if the practitioner is affiliated with a hospital or clinic, and if so, which one.

If you were involved in a major catastrophe such as an earthquake, flood, fire, or an event such as the Oklahoma City bombings or the World Trade Center attacks, there are usually organizations specifically geared to helping the victims of that particular tragedy.

If you are drawn to more alternative or complementary services, it can be a little trickier to find a practitioner. However, the following are some resources to help you get started. Also, you can often get very good information at your local health food store. Keep in mind that it is important to ensure that the practitioner is licensed, if applicable.

- Chiropractic—most insurance companies have a listing of licensed chiropractors in your area, or check at the website associationfornetwork care.com.
- Massage—some insurance companies list licensed massage therapists. Many physical therapy and chiropractic offices have massage therapists as well.
- Reiki, therapeutic touch, and hands-on healing—Reiki and therapeutic touch practitioners are certified, not licensed. For Reiki you can check the website of the International Center for Reiki Training (reiki.org/faq/whatisreiki.html). For therapeutic touch, check the Nurse Healers website at therapeutictouch.org. For hands-on healing, check with your spiritual counselor; many traditions offer this service.
- Acupuncture—some insurance companies list licensed acupuncturists. You can also check with your medical doctor or hospital or the website acufinder.com.
- Shamanic healing—shamanic healers are not legally licensed or certified. The Foundation for Shamanic Studies (shamanism.org) is one of the oldest and most reputable in this country. Sometimes indigenous shamans come to this country; this is a word-of-mouth network. The New York Shamanic Circle website (nyshamaniccircle.org) has information about reliable indigenous healers.
- Spiritual healing or counseling—contact your spiritual counselor or the California Institute of Integral Studies (ciis.edu/index.html).

- Homeopaths—some insurance companies will provide information for you, or you can visit the National Center for Homeopathy website at homeopathic.org.
- Herbalists—contact the American Herbalists Guild for information and referrals through its website (http://americanherbalistsguild.com).
- Ayurvedic practices—contact the National Institute of Ayurvedic Medicine at niam.com, or check in at your health food store.
- Meditation—your health food store should have information on meditation groups. You can also check Shambhala (shambhala.org), the Insight Meditation Society, Vipassana meditation (dharma.org), Zen meditation, or simply google "meditation" on the Internet.
- Peer support—twelve-step groups are available everywhere. You can contact the local chapter of Alcoholic Anonymous (AA) at the number listed in your phone directory or online at alcoholics-anonymous.org, and they will give you references to all kinds of twelve-steps groups. Your local library can help you as well.

Last, but not least, *trust yourself.* After you have made contact with a practitioner, make sure that person meets your expectations and that you feel comfortable with the practitioner and his or her office and staff. Make sure the practitioner is willing to spend the time with you that you need and that she or he is available to answer your questions in a way that makes sense to you.

And finally, of course, give yourself a hand for getting through this chapter! You might want to make a note of any decision that you've made with regard to treatment. But most important, take a self-care break. Do something lovely and nurturing for yourself before you go on with the rest of your day.

14

Trauma and Spirituality

Many people think of themselves as religious or spiritual, many do not. This chapter addresses the impact of trauma on a person's beliefs. What those beliefs are is not important for the purposes of this book. What matters is how they are altered or modified by a traumatic experience. This chapter focuses on what the shifts in beliefs and practices resulting from a trauma might be and aims to provide you with a road map of what these changes might look like and what to do about them.

At the onset, I want to emphasize that it is absolutely normal to

- Process and heal from a traumatic event within our customary frame of reference
- Have shifts in beliefs
- Have paranormal experiences

For some people their religious or spiritual beliefs inform their lives. Those beliefs dictate how they live, what they think about the world, and what, how, and when they eat, sleep, rest, make love, and so on. For others, spirituality is more an internal knowing that is not necessarily concretely expressed in their everyday lifestyle.

Trauma can upturn our whole belief system. For some, it becomes an opening into a spiritual or religious belief or practice. For others, it punctures and deflates a strongly held belief. Both responses are common. Sometimes the shift in beliefs is short-lived and, after the acute phase of the trauma, the person goes back to her or his original beliefs; for others, this shift becomes a life-changing perspective that continues to inform their lives after the impact of the trauma has been worked through and healed and life has returned to a sense of normalcy. For some, this shift will be abrupt and may feel uncomfortable. For others, it might simply evolve slowly and almost imperceptibly. As with most aspects of what we discuss in this book, there is no right or wrong—just your particular process, your particular path.

Another seldom-mentioned aspect of a traumatic experience is to have what is commonly referred to as a paranormal experience. Often those experiences make the person feel as if she or he is going crazy, or psychotic. During a paranormal experience people report seeing things or people that aren't there, sensing energy, seeing colors brighter than ever before, hearing voices that seem to come from nowhere, sensing angelic or ancestral presences, having heightened physical sensations such as hypersensitivity to heat, cold, or movement, or knowing things that they have no way of knowing. As one client reported, "It's like being on ayahuasca without taking anything."

Of course you need to check with a medical doctor to make sure that this is not a physiological manifestation of an injury or a reaction to a medication that you are taking as a result of your trauma. For example, Vito came to me after suffering a blow to his head that caused a serious concussion. A few weeks after the event, he started seeing stars at the periphery of his vision. He had gone to the doctor, who couldn't find anything wrong with him. Vito wasn't sure what was going on. He thought maybe this was the precursor to visions and that he was being called to sainthood, or as he said dryly, "Maybe I'm just going nuts!" I sent Vito to a vision specialist with a specialty in behavioral optometry. In one visit Vito was told that he wasn't going nuts, nor was he being called to sainthood. There was something in the way that his brain perceived the information that he received from his eyes that created this peripheral image of stars. Vito was fitted with refracting lenses, and his vision returned to normal.

Malka, on the other hand, discovered that she became clairvoyant after her trauma. She could see into people's bodies and knew what was wrong with them. She didn't quite know what to do or whom to talk to about it. Then, one day while in a bookstore, she found a book that had fallen on the floor. It was *Hands of Light* by Barbara Brennan, a renowned medical intuitive. Malka realized that she was able to diagnose people's diseases and decided to test out her ability. Timidly, she asked a doctor friend of hers whom she thought might be open to this if, with the patient's consent, she could sit in his consultation room. It turned out that Malka's diagnoses were always correct. She still is not sure what to do with her gift, and she won't tell many people about it, but at least she doesn't feel like she should check herself into the nearest hospital.

To some of the readers of this book this might sound like what my friend Corryn refers to as "California woo woo." However, it does happen, and if you might have experienced something of the kind, I want to reassure you that you are not going crazy. Emma Bragdon's book *The Call of Spiritual Emergency* is an excellent resource for those who may have had a paranormal experience. I want to encourage you—actually, I want to make a compelling request—to seek someone to talk with to help you through this experience. Finding the right practitioner will enable you to go through this time in a healthful way; not seeking help could land you in the psychiatric ward of the hospital.

Many, probably most, people do not experience a shift in their belief system. They maintain their religious or spiritual beliefs, or lack thereof, as they were before the traumatic event took place. That too is common and natural. Each person's process is unique, and you should not feel that you should have—or not have—a religious or spiritual experience because of having undergone a traumatic event.

How Trauma Can Affect Spirituality

Following are a few vignettes of how people's beliefs and lives were impacted by their traumatic experience. I have chosen rather extreme examples to illustrate the dramatic impact that a trauma can have on a person's religious or spiritual beliefs. However, most people who go through shifts do so in a much more subtle fashion. You might find yourself moving toward a house of worship or a spiritual practice, maybe return to one you had abandoned or neglected. Or you might find yourself becoming less involved in a habitual religious community or spiritual practice.

Benes had strong religious beliefs and a solid practice. He prayed every day, went to his house of worship for services, and followed the tenets of his faith. When he got hit by a shell in combat, he prayed. He prayed that he would be okay, that he wouldn't die. He didn't die, and although he was badly wounded he felt that God had been there with him. He felt grateful, and it deepened his devotional practice. He also felt that he wanted to do more to serve. He didn't quit his day job, but went to seminary to take courses. He now helps out teaching and leading retreats at his place of worship.

Veasna saw his friend being blown apart by a grenade as he lay a few feet away, unable to do anything. He was overwhelmed and terrified. He found himself starting to shake all over, and at the same time he experienced a sense of peace like he had never felt before. Veasna couldn't figure out what to do. He just lay there for what seemed to him like hours, shaking and feeling peaceful. Later on he was picked up and taken to the hospital. He was physically unharmed, and the doctors could not understand what the shaking was all about. He was treated for shock. At that point Veasna started hearing voices that told him that all would be well, not to worry, that he had had a spiritual awakening. He thought he was going crazy. A few weeks later he met Yemyo, who told him about yoga and kundalini experiences. Yemyo explained to Veasna that he was not going crazy, that he was experiencing a spiritual awakening in the form of what Yemyo called kundalini rising. There was nothing to worry about, but Veasna had to learn to manage this energy and work with it to incorporate the practice into his everyday life. (Many of the yoga styles cover kundalini rising experiences. The best known is the Yogi Bhajan tradition, with Gurmukh Khalsa being one of the principal teachers in the United States.)

Phillip, also a devout spiritual adherent, had a different experience, one that left him very shaken and confused. One day on his way to work he was brutally attacked by a gang of young men from a different religious persuasion. He prayed and prayed, but felt that it had been of no use. He was left on the sidewalk bleeding for what he felt was a long time before help came his way. He felt his God had abandoned him, and he could no longer believe. Although he recovered completely from his physical injuries, he never recovered from his loss of faith. Phillip felt that all he believed in had been lies. He went to speak with the elders of his spiritual community, but to no avail. His faith had been broken, and he could not recover it. It was a very difficult time for Phillip. He had relied on his faith and his community, and now he lost it all.

Leila, on the other hand, had been raised without any spiritual beliefs. Her parents were both scientists and believed in what could be proven and demonstrated, and God, spirits, an afterlife, and many other aspects of faith could not be proven, so they didn't believe in them. They believe in the right of all humans to live in peace and would never harm anything or anyone, but the mere mention of something that could not be observed and quantified was pure idiocy in their minds.

Like Malka, Leila was attacked on her way to work because "she didn't look right." Being dark skinned brought jeers and blows from a gang of white kids. She thought she was going to die. As she lay there, she felt that a force she could not describe had come to protect her and keep her alive, that it accompanied her to the hospital and through the surgeries, repeatedly letting her know that she would recover. Although she had no personal frame of reference to put her experience into context, she couldn't ignore it, and as much as she tried to rationalize it, it wouldn't go away. She wondered if she was being paranoid and going insane. What to do? Her parents and friends, though loving and supportive, would not in any way be able to be of assistance in this situation. Instinctively, Leila knew that going to a traditional psychiatrist would not be helpful, so she kept her experience to herself. The voice was still there telling her that all would be fine and that she would find the help that she needed. One day, she decided to go into a place of worship near where she lived. There was an old cleric there, and Leila felt drawn to him. She talked with him for a long time, and he helped her put her experiences in a context that made sense to her.

How Your Experience Affected Your Spirituality

The following exercises are designed to help you chart a course of discovery for yourself. I hope they will facilitate your coming to terms with any religious, spiritual, or paranormal experiences that might have occurred as a result of your traumatic event. Also, because our beliefs and actions impact other people (as we have covered in Chapters 10 and 11), there is an exercise about the effect of your shifts on others.

Take a moment to reflect on your spiritual or religious beliefs prior to your traumatic event. Write, draw, or make a collage to express those beliefs. You might also want to include quotations or symbols of the particular tradition you follow.

Take a moment to reflect on your spiritual or religious beliefs after your traumatic event. Write, draw, or make a collage that expresses your current beliefs. You might also want to include quotations or symbols.

Trauma and Spirituality

Your shift in spiritual or religious conviction may feel enjoyable and easy, or it may feel jarring and disquieting. It might be valuable for you to put down those aspects that feel positive, those that might feel negative, and those that are still unsorted in your mind. (Feel free to use pictures or symbols, write a poem or a song, create a dance, or make a sculpture if that is better for you than making a list.)

Positive Aspects	Negative Aspects	Unsorted Aspects

If you have negative or unsorted thoughts or feelings, you might want to consult a spiritual adviser of the religious or spiritual community or house of worship that either calls to you now or to which you have belonged in the past. There is no need to go through a religious or spiritual quandary or predicament on your own, and most spiritual advisers welcome inquiries. If that does not seem to be an appropriate venue, you might want to check with someone you trust or seek out a counselor or therapist who is willing to work with you on those issues. (Some possible resources are the California Institute for Integral Studies, the Association for Spirituality and Psychotherapy of the National Institute for the Psychotherapies in New York City, theological seminaries of any denomination, Common Boundary, the Foundation for Shamanic Studies, and the Institute of Noetic Sciences [noetic.org]. *The Call of Spiritual Emergency* by Emma Bragdon and *Spiritual Emergency* by Stanislav Grof have lots of good resources as well.)

If you are feeling overwhelmed and don't quite know where to start, refer to your support network from Chapter 12 and choose the person who might best be able to assist you in this task. Remember, that person does not necessarily have to be involved in a religious or spiritual group to be able to help you. He or she needs to be able to understand what it is that you are looking for and be a good detective to locate the best resource for you. You might choose to do both of the following exercises, or just one.

What spiritual questions do you have, and where can you go for assistance in finding answers?

Spiritual Issue   **Resources for Assistance**

_____   _____
_____   _____
_____   _____
_____   _____

If you had, or are having, a paranormal experience, the following exercises might help you sort out what is happening and help you figure out how to deal with it, what kind of support you might need, and where to get this support. Under each category, write any manifestation that applies.

Sight (clairvoyance): _____
_____
_____
_____

Hearing (clairaudient): _____
_____
_____
_____

Sensing (kinesthetic): _____
_____
_____
_____

Knowing (intuitive or psychic): _____

_____

_____

_____

Make a note of any symptom that you feel should be given medical attention. Like Vito earlier in the chapter, you might need to go see a vision specialist or a neurologist to make sure that there is no damage to your nervous system, and you might want to check any side effects of medication that you might be taking.

Symptom	What I Should Do
_____	_____
_____	_____
_____	_____
_____	_____

As with the preceding exercises, you don't have to do this alone. Refer to Chapter 12 to determine who the best person is to help you navigate this issue, whether by listening to you without judgment, helping you find the appropriate resource, or taking you to appointments.

What I Need	Who Can Help
_____	_____
_____	_____
_____	_____
_____	_____

Veasna, Malka, and Benes had powerful experiences, which they were able to incorporate without much impact on the rest of their lives, particularly their relationships with families and friends. In contrast, Phillip and Leila found themselves at odds with their families and friends. Leila's family and friends still accepted her for who she was, but she found that she had to keep a whole part of herself secret, and it made her feel as if she was living a double life. Over time they came to respect and accept her beliefs, though that area of their relationship remained tenuous and somewhat strained. Phillip's family could not accept that he no longer wanted to participate in the spiritual practices that dominated their lives. After a while he moved away, and he felt as if he had been excommunicated from his whole community. It was very difficult for him.

You might have had some spiritual experience similar to those of the people mentioned in this chapter. However, your experience most likely was more of a gentle modification of what your beliefs and practices had been prior to your trauma. Regardless, it might have impacted those close to you. The following exercises offer you an opportunity to determine what that impact was and what, if anything, you need to do about it.

People who might have been affected by my spiritual or religious shift:

Person   **How He or She Was Affected**

Spouse/partner   _____

Children   _____

Parents   _____

Siblings   _____

Other relatives:

_____   _____

_____   _____

_____   _____

Friends:

_____   _____

_____   _____

_____   _____

_____   _____

Coworkers:

_____   _____

_____   _____

_____   _____

_____   _____

☞ *Write, draw, and/or make a collage of how you feel about these people's reactions.*

☞ *What, if anything, do you need to do about it? Possibly, like Phillip, you might need to move away from your family and community of friends, or more likely, like Leila, you might be able to open conversations that will lead to a renewed understanding between you. Take some time to write or draw what needs to happen.*

I hope that this chapter has brought you comfort and helped you feel that, although no one has exactly the same experience as someone else, you are not alone and your experience is normal. It might have been difficult for you to revisit some painful or scary ground. It might be sad to note that some relationships and ways of life may have ended. It might have been reassuring and exhilarating to find out that other people have had experiences similar to yours.

If you are dealing with difficult questions related to this topic, make sure to seek the appropriate support. You deserve it. Now, take a few minutes to be gentle and caring with yourself. Breathe, relax, do something lovely for yourself before you go on with your day.

15

Gratitude

"Great suffering brings great compassion."

—from a Vietnamese poem

Whether or not we've gone through a traumatic experience, there are so many things most of us can be grateful for. For the most part, though, we tend take the things that we have for granted.

Many years ago, during a very difficult period in my own life, I was introduced to a gratitude practice. At the time I felt that I didn't have much to feel grateful about. As far as I was concerned, my life was falling apart. But I decided that I had nothing to lose. Every evening I named ten things I was grateful for. At first I didn't exactly love doing this, and I would struggle to find ten things—sometimes I didn't. Sometimes it was simply that I had enough food that day, or that I was not cold, or that a friend had called. However I was persistent, I kept at it, and slowly it became easier and I began to notice that there was always more to be grateful for than I realized.

I believe that this gratitude practice was one of the pivotal things that helped get me out of the darkness. It was a wonderful lesson in learning to focus on the positives, and I learned that no matter how dark the night, there can be a ray of light. Twenty-some years later, I still do it every night.

This is my invitation to you: look at the silver lining of your trauma. You have gone through a trauma, and you are on the other side of it. As we have contemplated throughout this book, you have had to face many challenges and difficulties since your traumatic experience, and you may still be dealing with some of the ramifications. Nonetheless, going through a trauma can bring great gifts. Sometimes those gifts are internal and come in the form of a new perspective on life or a new sense of purpose. Other times the gifts are external and come in the response we get from others, an acknowledgment of how much we are cared about.

Darshan was at Ground Zero when the World Trade Center was attacked. Because he happened to stop for coffee on his way to work, right before the first plane crashed, he survived without a scratch. He's not quite sure what propelled him to get coffee, because he is not usually a coffee drinker. He still talks about feeling so grateful for his life, and feeling grateful that he feels grateful. Darshan had had a pretty easy life. Good home, good schools, good opportunities, good job, friends. He had it all, and he was doing well—and took it pretty much for granted. Now he still has it all, but he also has an appreciation for what he has, and that has made it all the sweeter.

Paloma recently was in a terrible car accident. When she came to talk to me about it, she was filled with gratitude for the outpouring of support that she had received from her friends. She was awed by the number of people who called and offered help. It taught her that there are many people who care about her and are willing to be of help, that she is not alone in the world.

Just today an acquaintance was telling me that she had recently been diagnosed with a terminal illness. Miki had had a tough life, and she just now had come to a place of ease. At first she was quite upset, angry, and despondent, then she decided that she still had a life to live and that she wanted to live it fully. "Now I'm grateful for the warmth and beauty of the sunshine. I never used to notice," she said, "and I'm going to see those I love more often."

Practicing Gratitude

The following exercises provide some ideas to help you to develop your own gratitude practice. I encourage you to take a separate piece of paper for each question and keep adding as you think of new things that you are grateful for.

People

Make a list of the people in your life you are grateful for. You can also write why you are grateful for them, which is a nice thing to do but not necessary; it's plenty to recognize that person and her or his value in your existence. You can name people in your present or people from your past who made an impact, even if you haven't had any contact with them for years. I'm still grateful for Mr. Bean, who in the sixth grade found a way to keep me interested in school.

Name   **Why You Are Grateful**

_____   _____
_____   _____
_____   _____
_____   _____
_____   _____
_____   _____
_____   _____
_____   _____
_____   _____
_____   _____
_____   _____
_____   _____

Carlos loves to run, and he loves to compete. To tell the truth, Carlos lives for sports, for movement! While serving a tour of duty in a combat zone, Carlos caught a piece of shrapnel in his knee. He was stunned that this had happened to him. How could it? After all, he's a runner. Things like that don't happen to runners! But there it was, a blown knee. At first he thought he might lose his knee altogether. Fortunately, the doctors were able to rebuild his knee, and after a lot of physical therapy and rehabilitation, Carlos can now move almost as smoothly as anyone—but he can't run. Carlos was furious and scared—furious that his fun was taken away from him, scared because a great deal of his sense of identity was connected to his running successes.

Carlos was encouraged to begin a gratitude practice—one specifically focused on the gifts of his trauma. Needless to say, he wasn't exactly thrilled at the idea. Finally he grudgingly agreed to give it a try. We settled on one thing a day, and he could repeat the same thing more than one day. Carlos was amazed. After a relatively short time he had a long list of gratitudes. To his surprise, the biggest gift was an appreciation and a sense of compassion for other people's pain. He felt it made him so much more understanding and caring of people, and it enhanced his relationships with family and friends.

Write the things that you are grateful for in your life, today or from the past. It doesn't have to be big or complicated: for example, you could be grateful that there is water coming out of your faucet, that you have food and shelter, for your job, for your financial well-being, and so on.

Things you are grateful for:

_____

_____

_____

_____

_____

_____

_____

_____

_____

_____

_____

_____

_____

_____

_____

_____

As we go through a difficult time, we also become aware of or develop qualities that help us make it through the hardships and their aftermath (including making it through this book, which is no small task!).

For example, Carlos came to appreciate his motivation to do the work to walk again and his ability to look at his feelings about his ordeal and to work through the emotional pain that accompanied it while keeping a sense of humor. He even came to appreciate his willingness to do the gratitude practice. Vinny, in Chapter 13, was grateful for his stubborn streak that wouldn't allow him to quit even when he was in such despair that he thought he wouldn't get better, and for his capacity to remain loving and gentle.

Take some time to write down the qualities you appreciate about yourself. Don't be shy—after all, no one has to see it!

Qualities I appreciate in myself:

There is one more gratitude practice I'd like to offer you. Find a beautiful box or make one (shoe boxes can be beautifully decorated), or create a lovely folder marked "Gratitudes." Whenever you feel grateful for something, write it down and put it in the box or folder. Then, when you are feeling blue and despondent, open the box and look at all the things you can be grateful for. It's a good reminder that the sun is always there, even when we can't see it.

You can use the same technique with a box or folder called "Appreciation." In it put anything that anyone sends you or tells you about how they appreciate you or your work in some way. On bad days, pull it out. You'll feel better!

Staying Grateful

This chapter might have been bittersweet. The bitter part: you might have gotten in touch with certain ways of thinking that are a bit uncomfortable, or it might have touched some parts of yourself that feel ungrateful or those areas of your life where there is not much to feel gratitude for. The sweet part: I hope that you were able to note all the people and things that you can be grateful for, that you were able to bring some gentleness and compassion to yourself, and that you now have a new tool to bring some peace and comfort into your life, no matter what is going on.

Take a moment to savor the positive. Anchor it with a small ritual or ceremony, whether it is drinking a cup of coffee, taking a bath, going for a walk, or whatever will feel gentle and nurturing.

16

Looking Forward

"Everything must change, nothing stays the same."
—from a Hebrew song

Life is like a river, always changing. Some changes are subtle, others more dramatic; some are welcomed, others not so. Trauma is like a huge boulder that drops in the middle of life's path. It forces you to alter the usual pattern of your life's flow. Trauma requires that you adapt and adjust to new challenges and circumstances. Sometimes trauma demands adjustments that are enormous. Sometimes the adaptations are minor, perhaps even imperceptible. Nevertheless, one thing is certain: you cannot go through a trauma unmarked.

This book has encouraged you to explore areas of your life that may have been impacted by your trauma: your health, your relationships, your work, your mental well-being, your perspective on life. This chapter aims to provide you with an overview of the changes that have taken place in your life since your trauma. Some of these changes may be big, others seemingly unimportant. Several of these changes you might like, several others not.

As you go through the following exercises, I invite you to consider the many ways that trauma has impacted your life and your sense of self. The changes in your life may be positive and life enhancing. For example, Maeko found that after her trauma she reconnected with her spiritual practice that she had ignored for many years, Malik took the time to go bicycling, George chose to be more focused on his work, Ebony started calling her parents once a week, Carlos started a gratitude practice, Denali went for a complete overhaul—she cut her hair, started wearing makeup, and bought a new, more flattering wardrobe—and Raphael bought a house and got married.

> *List the positive changes in your life since your trauma. Remember that they all matter, no matter how small.*

You may have taken certain positive actions as a consequence of your trauma. Some may have become an integral part of who you are. Others you might find dwindling over time, like forgetting to take time for yourself now that you are no longer in pain. Somehow you find yourself returning to your old ways of being. It is common for all of us to do that. However, it is important to maintain your positive habits, even when you are over the hump, because those are the aspects of our life that keep us connected and engaged. For example, Quana went on a healthy diet and exercise regime after she had a mild stroke. Fortunately she recovered well and was able to resume her normal life. Slowly she started working overtime again, didn't exercise much, and ate whatever she found. The last time she went to the doctor, her blood pressure was high, as was her cholesterol. Quana was smart enough to realize the damage she was doing to herself and went back to a healthier lifestyle.

_____
_____
_____
_____
_____
_____
_____
_____
_____

On the other hand, your trauma may have brought about negative changes in your life, changes that have hindered or impeded the expected flow of your life. For example, Eduardo, who was wounded in the war, found himself confined to a wheelchair. Jacqui's young husband also died in battle, leaving her with a young baby. She never expected to be a single parent and was having a hard time adjusting to what she felt would be a lonely life. Gladys was devastated by the loss of her home in a flood. She couldn't imagine ever finding a place to live that she liked as much as where she had grown up and then raised her children, where she felt like part of a community.

List the negative changes in your life that have resulted from your trauma, whether they are practical or emotional.

_____
_____
_____
_____
_____
_____

_____

_____

_____

_____

_____

_____

This list must have been difficult to make, and it might have made you feel even worse about your situation. However, I'm an incorrigible optimist, and as I've said throughout this book, I believe that there is always hope. You don't have to be stuck in the negatives.

It is true that some of the alterations in your life may be irreversible. For example, Eduardo will most likely never walk again, and Jacqui will not get her husband back. Of course, if you suffer a loss you must go through the stages of grief, but then there comes a time when you must go on with your life. There are actions you can take that will make even the most difficult situation bearable.

The following image has helped me and many others in situations like this: Imagine that your life is a glass that has broken. With patience, you can pick up the pieces and put them back together with lead to create a goblet—in the way that stained glass is put together. The result is a goblet in which some of the original pieces are missing, but the core is still there—in a new, stronger, and equally beautiful form.

Like Kevin and Carlos, you can turn your situation into a positive. One way is to heighten your awareness of your negative patterns. Once you realize what your thoughts, feelings, and behaviors are that don't work, you can consciously choose to make a change. This is easier said than done, so you might want to seek out guidance from a relative, a friend, or a professional who can help you in your quest to deal with those aspects of your life and their reverberations.

What do you think you could do to reverse your negative patterns or behaviors? As you do this exercise, remember that it doesn't have to be big. And sometimes it is close to miraculous. Olivia felt all alone in the world. Her brother, her only living relative, had recently died in combat. One morning she got into the subway, and an old man handed her some wildflowers and said, "Isn't a glorious day" and gave her a radiant smile. Olivia thanked him, sat down, and closed her eyes for what she thought was a brief moment. When she opened them, the old man was gone. But all of a sudden she no longer felt alone in the world—she no longer felt that no one would ever care for her again.

Patterns

_____
_____
_____
_____
_____
_____
_____
_____
_____
_____

What You Can Do

_____
_____
_____
_____
_____
_____
_____
_____
_____

Looking Forward

✎ Write, draw, and/or make a collage of the possibilities opened to you. What can you do to go over or around the boulder of your trauma and find a new path for the flow of your life?

Experiencing a trauma often affects your perspective on life. What seemed important at one time is no longer so, and conversely, aspects of your life that may have been neglected become more pressing or meaningful. Write, draw, and/or make a collage of how your perspective on life has changed since your trauma. Again, it doesn't have to be a humongous change. Often the most subtle things are the most powerful, like Olivia realizing that she was not all alone in the world.

Remember, life is always full of possibilities, not always probabilities, but the possibilities are infinite. Let yourself dream. An old shaman friend always says, "If you can dream it, you can make it happen . . . or at least something like it."

A Final Note

危机

This Chinese pictograph for *crisis* depicts both the character for danger and the character for opportunity. You have survived the danger, and you have taken the steps on your journey to healing. At this time, I invite you to congratulate yourself for the hard work you have put into recovery and this workbook. It took courage and perseverance.

I hope that reflecting on your trauma and its aftermath, reverberations, and ramifications has allowed you to acknowledge and honor what you experienced, both at the time of the trauma and afterward. Honor the coping skills that you have developed, the changes that you went through, and the adjustments and adaptations you have had to make to forge ahead with your life. I also hope that you are feeling more accepting and compassionate toward yourself in your ongoing process of healing.

Write, draw, and/or make a collage of your healing journey.

Finally, I encourage you to do something wonderful and celebratory for yourself. You might want to create a ceremony of completion, go to dinner with close friends or someone you love, write a note to yourself, go for a lovely hike—or any of the multitude of ways that will honor and recognize your healing journey.

May you walk with Beauty before you

May you walk with Beauty behind you

May you walk with Beauty on either side of you

May you walk with Beauty below you

May you walk with Beauty above you

May you walk in Beauty

—*Native American blessing*

Healing from Post-Traumatic Stress

Index

Child pose, 13
Chiropractors, 161

D

Daydreams, 83
   exercise for, 89, 90
   working with, 86–87
Dreams, 81–83
   exercise for, 88, 90
   journals for, 87–91
   working with, 84–87

E

Emotional well-being, 154–59
Events. *See* Traumatic events
Exercises
   for acknowledging sorrow/sadness, 73
   for anger/resentment, 76
   for asking for help, 141–42, 145–47
   for charting future, 188–89
   for dreams/nightmares, 89, 90
   for expressing thoughts, 73
   for feelings, 20, 26–27
   for guilt, 56–57
   for impact of trauma on people close to you, 131
   for interests, hobbies, activities, 120
   for loss, 72
   for place of residence, 112
   for practicing gratitude, 178–82

F

Family, impact of trauma on, 128–36
Feelings
   common, after traumatic events, 18–19
   exercise for making collage of, 20, 26–27
   of others, dealing with, 77–78
   relaxation techniques for, 10–11
Fetal position, 13
Fight, flight, freeze reactions, 41–51
Flashbacks, 83–84
   exercise for, 89, 90
   working with, 86–87
Forgiveness, of oneself, 57–59
Friends, impact of trauma on, 128–36
Future
   exercises for, 188–89
   looking toward, 183–88

G

Gratitude, 177–78
   practicing, exercises for, 178–82
Grief, 69–71
   anger and, 75
   expressing, 79–80
   understanding other people's, 77–78
Guilt, 53–55
   exercise for, 56–57

H

Hands of Light (Brennan), 164–65
Healing process, self-care and, 7
Help
   asking for, 138–48
   exercises for, 141–42, 145–47
Herbalists, 162
Hobbies, 118–26
   exercise for, 120
Homeopaths, 162
Homes
   checklist for, 113–17
   exercise for, 112
   trauma and, 110–18